THE BALANCE OF
LIFE

THE BALANCE OF
LIFE

TRUST | RESPECT | SAFETY | COMMUNICATION

GERARD BROWN, MS ED. MFT

TATE PUBLISHING & Enterprises

Published by Tate Publishing & Enterprises, LLC
127 E. Trade Center Terrace | Mustang, Oklahoma 73064 USA
1.888.361.9473 | www.tatepublishing.com

Tate Publishing is committed to excellence in the publishing industry. The company reflects the philosophy established by the founders, based on Psalm 68:11,
"The Lord gave the word and great was the company of those who published it."

Book design copyright © 2010 by Tate Publishing, LLC. All rights reserved.
Cover design by Leah LeFlore
Interior design by Joey Garrett

Published in the United States of America

ISBN: 978-1-61739-052-4
1. Family & Relationships / Interpersonal Relations
2. Family & Relationships / General
10.09.09

"WITH HOPE, YOU HAVE A PRESENT AND FUTURE."

—G. BROWN

DEDICATION

This book is dedicated to all those that have been helped in the counseling process as well as those that have opened their hearts to learning how to change themselves so they can affect change in others.

It is also dedicated to those in the counseling profession that take into their own hearts those that they are charged to help. Not everyone can be a counselor; it takes a very special person with a caring nature, sharp mind, big heart, and the ability to guide those that are usually desperate for a positive growth in their lives. To be a counselor is more than a profession it's a lifetime commitment. They are people usually chosen by divine guidance to be of service to others.

ACKNOWLEDGEMENTS

This book has been a labor of love. It took much longer for me to do it than I thought it would. Not because of a lack of information, but from my own need to be sure I provided all that is necessary information for the reader to make positive choices in their lives.

First, I would like to thank my wife, Margaret, for her support, input, patience, and love. She was my inspiration. She has lived a very hard life, but she has a childlike faith and a genuine love of and for people. She kept on me to do this book as well as continuing to grow in my own career as a husband, father, therapist, and counselor. She has been my rock.

Next, I would like to thank my stepson, Nick, for all he has taught me. He has grown into a man and moving forward in a positive way. It was because of his challenges to me as a child that I chose this field. He showed me how to be tough and yet gentle when you have to be. His heart is his mother's, and his spirit is his. Chase those dreams, Nick, but try to keep your head focused on the real and attainable goals in life.

I would like to thank Shannon Marie; she is my miracle baby. She supported me and has been an inspiration to my writing as well as my counseling. She is the ultimate listener. She has a heart of gold that is as pure as the driven snow. She gets her sassiness from her mother and her contemplation from me; she is a deep thinker and a true friend.

I would like to thank all those that said, "I want this book," or "I need this book—get it done!" Thank you, Uncle Frank and Aunt Margaret. You have both been my never ending fountain of joy and support. Thank you Vicki in Georgia; your artistic talents on cover ideas have inspired me to work even harder. Thank you Nancy for you input and sharp eye. To Leslie, Debby, Carole, Eileen, Sonia, Carolyn, Dana, Erik, Tina, Megan, Tom, and above all, Dr. Erwin Maseelall, who kept me going medically and supported me all the way. His loving philosophy to us all is "If it tastes good, spit it out." I am sure I probably missed a few friends, but they know I appreciate them and their love and support for me and this book.

Thank you, to all my past and present clients. You presented your problems for help, but you are really a teacher to those that haven't taken or had the chance to go to therapy. I continue to pray a prayer of thanks for each of you daily.

I also need to thank God, for His Divine inspiration, leadership, and a path that I was driven to follow. Sometimes I am stubborn, but His patience is everlasting. Thank you for helping me to stand strong in adversity. Thank you for placing people in my life that have unshakeable faith. Thank you for bringing the clients to my door.

TABLE OF CONTENTS

INTRODUCTION

Wen writing this book, I wondered if I had come across a new way of looking at an old problem. How do we get along as humans? How do we keep relationships together? How do we survive disagreements? How do we fix what has been broken? How do we learn to love again?

In our society, it is so convenient to just walk away from families, relationships, peers, life, etc. Today we catch ourselves divorcing all that we hold dear if it doesn't go the way we want. So many clients give up because of minute differences. I have worked with children that have emotionally divorced their parents because they didn't get their way. It is always amazing to me how easily we quit. It seems it is so easy for us to do. We are a society that has become so disposable and desensitized to life and love that we just shut it off and feel nothing for walking away.

We have grown up with video games that teach us to kill, wound, maim, and destroy what is in front of us. We have been educated by television, movies, and other media that is so easily accessible. Most media we encounter today has the ability to teach us over and over to just quit and move on if we don't get our way. Without a doubt, we, as individuals and families, have lost what it means to have unity and love. The truth is we need to understand what it is that we are really doing and what causes us to do it.

Take a moment; visualize yourself sitting at a strong, yet beautiful, four-legged table. When you are at this table you know the table is strong, stable, and most of all balanced. Imagine if the table had one leg, would it fall? It probably would. How about two legs? It may be a little stable, but would need support to stabilize. If it had three legs, it may stand alone, but could be very unstable. If it has four legs, it is usually strong, balanced, and can support a large amount of weight. What I will present in this book are the ways to recognize if one leg or more is missing and ways to balance your table, or life, with complete support and reinforcement. This table will be well balanced and very strong. It will be able to withstand an enormous amount of weight and abuse.

We as a society have become busy, stressed, and overwhelmed; we have lost sight of what it takes to have balance in our lives. We move too fast and ignore what could be hurting us in ways that will take years or a lifetime to fix. Your family may have love, but is it balanced, stable, and safe?

In order to balance our lives and love, we have to understand what parts must be included to make this happen.

I have found that in order to have a solid yet well balanced relationship with self as well as others, there must be a minimum of four equally balanced legs.

A leg is a limb serving as a means of support to a structure. The names of these legs of support are safety, respect, trust, and communication.

Safety is the condition of being safe, freedom from danger, risk, or injury. Safety is a device designed to prevent accidents.

Respect is to feel or show regard for esteem. Respect also means to avoid violation or interference as well as to show concern.

Trust is to have firm reliance on the integrity, ability, or character of a person or thing. It is also something committed into the care of another. One in which confidence is placed. Without trust we have no future to base hope upon.

Communication is the exchange of thoughts, messages, or information, as by speech, signals, writing, or behavior. Communication is a system of sending or receiving messages.

THE BALANCE OF LIFE

By understanding how each of these balance plus how they interact, one can work to rebuild or continue on the path of wholeness as a couple, family, and self. If we understand how each look, we will know what areas need to be worked on. It is my hope and prayer that after reading this book you will be able to balance and stabilize your life, your relationships, and our world on a firm foundation rather than a foundation of ever moving and shifting sand. You will also be able to help others in the path to wholeness, but only after you are healthy and in charge of yourself.

Know that you cannot be of any help to anyone if you aren't healthy yourself. In order to attain this stable health, you must learn to be *selfish*. Being selfish isn't being stingy. It means to baby yourself until you are feeling and being healthy in your decisions and life choices.

THE BALANCE
OF SAFETY

afety is the condition of being safe, freedom from danger, risk, or injury. Safety is a device designed to prevent injury.

Safety is the feeling of being away from danger.

Is everything safe? Is your home, your work, or your life in general always safe? Do you feel safe with the decisions you make in your life? Are you very comfortable with all that is going on around you? Are you safe with your mate? Are you safe with your family, friends, and acquaintances? Or, do you feel unsafe, ill at ease, and uncomfortable most of the time? I would imagine the last may be more true than not. These questions are there for you to evaluate how you feel in your environment, be it at home, work, or anywhere. By answering these questions honestly, you will be able to evaluate what you may need to work on. Using your brain as a tool of measurement is good, but learning to use your heart as your guide will give you a much more stable way to judge because your heart isn't filled with conflict and judgments. As you read and practice the interventions in this book you will see how your brain and heart can work independently in decision making.

The other day, I was walking toward my car in a local mall parking lot. As I reached into my pocket for my keys, I felt on the key pad for the six buttons—remote start, lock, unlock, gas cap cover, trunk release, and panic button that makes the horn blow, the lights flash, and I don't know what else. I found myself staring at the pad and trying to make sure I hit the right button. I can't tell you all the times I thought I hit the door unlock and my trunk opened or my gas cap cover flew open. To further embarrass myself, the alarm went off, and everyone in the neighborhood looked to see what the ruckus was all about. I am becoming more and more paranoid that I will hit the wrong button. I thought to myself, *safety!* What have we, as a society, come too? My vehicle will not start unless I have the right coded key. When I get in, I have "idiot lights" to remind me to wear my seat belt; close my door; and fill up on fuel, oil, and even window washer fluid. Heaven forbid the check engine light comes on. That is when panic really hits, and your safety may be at risk.

If I were to get into an accident, my car has safety restraints that engage in a millisecond to protect me and my passengers. If I am backing up, a beep or a voice goes off alerting me if I am getting too close to something. I even have a system that if I get to close or someone is too close to me, the vehicle will adjust distance automatically to ensure safety. I don't have to look on a map anymore. I have a global positioning system (GPS) to tell me where to turn, when to turn, and about any problems I may encounter on the way. I have a phone system in my vehicle that I can use (hands free) that will tell me what is wrong with my vehicle. This system will also tell me how to get an emergency handled by connecting me to the emergency number. *Safety!*

As I drove, I noticed street lights, stop lights, warning signs, speed limit signs, lines in the road, and orange barrels for construction to make things safer. When I turned into my driveway, my outside driveway/yard light turned on to brighten my way. I then push my automatic garage door button (with automatic safety stop in case a child or an animal obstructs its operation) the door raised and I drove my car in to the well lit garage. So I don't pull to close to the wall there is an automatic red light that tells me I am in far enough. I turned off my car, and the buzzer reminds me to take my keys out of the ignition. The timed headlights are on for a few seconds to light my way so I don't trip on my way in. I put my key into the entrance door, open the door and rush in to turn off my home security alarm, and then I take a deep breath. I am home safe and sound as my voice-activated lights turn on in my home, my stereo started to played softly, my laptop signaled I had mail, and my answering machine voiced I had numerous messages.

Wouldn't it be nice if our lives had these fail-safes? In many ways they do: We have laws, family rules, personal rules, and boundaries.

Safety is a severe issue when it comes to abuse. Abuse happens in three ways:

1. Physical Abuse
2. Sexual Abuse
3. *Emotional Abuse*

All three are devastating to the victim and anyone around the abuse—for example, your children. All three leave scars that don't just go away. I will elaborate on Physical and Sexual abuse here and Emotional abuse in a later chapter.

Physical Abuse: Causing injury to another by hitting, restraining, or other means of injury.

I had one client whose husband was a pro at this. He would hit his wife in the buttocks, ribs, thighs, head at the hairline, or any other place that couldn't be easily seen. He hit her any time she didn't comply with his demands. As time went on, all he had to do was act like he was going to hit her, and she would comply. Have you ever seen a dog that was abused? All you have to do is look at them or talk harshly, and they cower. This is exactly what this client looked like. She took this abuse for a few years because she was too afraid to call the authorities. When asked by her family what was going on, she would laugh it off. She expressed how clumsy she was when they noticed a mark. As time went on, her spouse became more creative in his abuse. He would lock her in a room in the house and not allow her to eat, sleep, or even go to the bathroom without his approval. At one point, he locked her in a room under the porch for hours to days. He would isolate her from her parents and friends. He became the ultimate bully and she was the perfect victim.

She finally had enough when his young children, from three previous marriages, started to hurt her as well. They would taunt, belittle, and hit her. Finally, when one of them tried to burn her with a heated fork, she packed her bags, went to a women's shelter, and sought help. If it wasn't for her seeking help from a trusted friend, she would have probably been in the abusive relationship today or until she lost her life.

This woman had a normal family upbringing. She was taught by the example of her church-going parents to be kind and loving. To her the most important role in life was taking care of others. Her parents were married many years and were pillars of the community. Her dad was very loving, yet very strict as his dad was. He believed sparing the rod spoils the child. He was much closer to his son than his two girls. Her mom was raised with traditional family norms and values: the man is the head of the house, and she was to do her wifely role at all times. She was raised to be very subservient to the husband. She catered to the men of the house and raised her girls to do the same. When her dad spoke, all listened. The men of the family were fed first. When they had their fill the men retired to the den to discuss or watch sports. The men participated in sports at very early ages. The men were very competitive with each other. They never invited the women to participate with them, but they could be quiet observers. The men never did any "women's" chores. She was an easy target for abuse.

What does a physically abused person or target look like?

I am sure in your lifetime you may have seen or heard about a person that has been physically abused. They are usually pretty easy to pick out. They look two ways.

A) Mean, gruff, aggressive, a fighter. They will take nothing from anybody and strike first before they are struck. Their goal is to not be hurt and/or keep their hurt to a minimum. They usually fight dirty and will use any force necessary to stop their opponent.

One of my male clients was an ex-marine, married, and had two children. He had a severe drinking problem but was proud to say he had not used drugs much. He had a prison record for assault and battery and had been in jail for numerous driving under the influence of alcohol or drugs. He even boasted that he once was in a jail cell next to his dad, who was charged with killing his mother. He was self-described as your typical "bad boy." He thought of himself as a "chick magnet" and had numerous extra-marital affairs.

After meeting with him on several occasions, he started to trust me and told me about his upbringing. He was severely abused by his family. His dad would hang him in the garage by his arms and beat him with his leather belt. The more he cried, the more he got beat. He eventually was able to stop crying and take it like a man. His mother would beat him as well. As a child he had enuresis, which means he wet the bed. When his mom caught him, she would beat him and put him on the front porch to stand nude. She would then drape the soiled bedclothes over his head until she came and got him, which could be , many hours later. His friends would walk by, see him, and taunt him. They only quit after he "beat them all down." His wife described him as quick-tempered and said he only hit her once in a while. She said, he would never hit the kids, just scream like a Drill Sergeant at them face-to-face, nose-to-nose, or make them stand in the corner of the closet for an hour or so. They didn't see this type behavior as abusive; both had been raised this way. When I confronted them regarding child social services, they terminated counseling immediately, saying that they felt better and would call me when they needed me. I learned from a social agency they had moved to another state.

B) The other way that an abuse victim looks may be as a terrified, withdrawn person or as one that loves to laugh and make others laugh around them. They usually don't trust anyone, or could be people that have weak boundaries and allow others to victimize them.

I worked with a lady who was one of six sisters. She was raised in a middle-class neighborhood by a dad that provided support for her and a mom that was an addictive socialite. At a very young age, she was told by her mom that she didn't like her and that she would never amount to anything. This young lady felt very unsafe around her mother and was treated to both emotional as well as forms of physical abuse as a child and through her teen years. At eighteen years old, she ran from the home to another state. She wanted to go to college to prove her mom wrong. That would have been fine, except she met a guy that kept up the abuse, and he believed in keeping her barefoot and pregnant. She had two kids in a very short time. The husband left her to raise the kids and he move on to his next victim.

This young lady married and divorced three more times before she decided to seek therapy and learn to recognize the *poison* that she kept ingesting.

If I were to pick a movie that had a physically abused person portrayed, I would choose the movie *Enough* (2002) by Columbia Pictures, starring Jennifer Lopez. She was brutally abused in this portrayal. She started to look the part until she had enough. She took the initiative to train herself to defend herself against her tormentors.

This is a prime example of how to take charge of self and affect change in the situation. The change in this character and her perception of the danger she faced affected the change in the abuser. The way she presented to others is the way she was perceive by them. When she presented herself as a victim that is how the bullies saw her. When she presented herself positive and strong that is how she was seen. She went from being a victim to a survivor because of the changes she made in herself.

Sexual Abuse: being violated without choice, being sexually taken advantage of by one person or another, as by the use of threats or cohersion.

Volumes have been written on sexual abuse. This is probably the most demeaning abuse that can be done to a human being. This abuse removes freedom, trust, integrity, joy, and much more. This abuse is in many ways unforgivable, yet alone unforgettable. When this abuse happens to people the emotional and sometimes physical scars run deep. The feelings of revenge are just as deep, even if not played out. It is amazing to me how many times this topic comes up mostly in women, but it has in men as well.

This is an abuse that affects the physical body, which in turn affects everything else. I have had a client as young as five-years-old who was raped by a trusted neighbor boy, to a senior citizen who was raped by her trusted uncle. Sexual abuse is devastating. It takes a very long time to help this victim, and that is if they can even talk about it. All abuse victims have one thing in common. They have had their *trust* of others removed, and the abuse is traumatic, problematic, and most times can cause somatic issues in others ways.

I had one client who was highly respected in the community, held numerous high-level jobs, advanced degrees, and was a person that most people would look up to and envy. He called me to just talk. He said he kept having dreams that would turn into nightmares. He would wake up soaking wet with sweat, crying, shivering, and trembling. He saw faces, but they weren't recognizable. They were monsters, both males and females. The nightmares were happening more often. It used to be once in awhile, now it was almost each night. He found he hated going to bed. He would stay up at night until he had to sleep. He was breaking out in itchy red bumps all over his body. He was becoming hyper-vigilant all the time where he felt people were following him. He constantly looked behind him and felt his colleagues were plotting to get him.

We started talking about these dreams. One thing led to another, and the next thing I knew, he was telling me how much he hated his dad, mom, sister, aunt, grandmother, uncle, and numerous others who, as a child sexually abused him, beat him, and even tried to murder him. He suffered from a personality disorder that eventually caused him to resign from his career. He became paralyzed in fear. He couldn't go anywhere, see anyone, or even talk about what his brain was showing him. He described it as his forehead having doors on it. Behind each door was something bad that had happened in his life. One night, as he lay in bed trying to go to sleep, all the doors opened at one time. His emotional pictures took him to the pits of hell. He was devastated; all he could do was wail and cry. He spent days in bed, not eating, sleeping, or talking, just crying. He described it as if his guts were torn out. All of his emotions were erased and rage was put in its place.

He found that in order to cope from the past he would bury the situations behind doors in his head. To cope, he would take on other personalities during and after the abuses. Today, after years of intense therapy by professionals in this field, he is doing much better. He still is on disability, and will most likely be the rest of his life, but he has started to find ways to become whole again. He has had to address the nightmares and the personalities one at a time; they were poison to him. He also has had to put closure to those that hurt him. Many of them are deceased now, yet he had to do interventions that helped him heal. He wrote letters that he took to the cemeteries and left at their graves. He has shredded numerous pictures, letters, cards, etc. He has gone to some who are still alive to confront them or sent letters to them. He has in many ways done all he can without getting himself in legal trouble. He is still working on his closure daily, and probably will the rest of his life. One important catharsis is that he now can admit he was a victim and is now a survivor. He feels better about himself. He still carries the physical and emotional scars. He can't be in public places for long, or with groups (even trusted friends). He still suffers severe anxiety and panic manifesting itself. But, he has learned coping skills to help himself get through the traumas of each day. He states he can see light at the end of the tunnel. Yet the tunnel is long and at times terrifyingly dark.

One of the key elements here is *finding closure*. I advise my clients that in order to move on they must put closure to the trauma that brought them to be stuck. There are numerous therapeutic interventions that can help to do this. Here are just a few.

Write a note, letter, or volumes about the issues to the perpetrator. It doesn't have to be perfect, just start writing. If you have trouble starting draw small circles on the paper until you start writing. It is like priming the pump. Don't worry about spelling, language, or even bad words if they come out. All you are trying to do is get the pain out of your insides and on to the paper. You want to empty your head and all the wasted space that the pain and poison has taken up. The closure for this writing is whatever you want to do with it. Some clients hide it for a while, then get it out and read it to see if they feel the same as they did.

Rip it up. Bury it. Burn it. Shred it. One client tied it to a few helium balloons and let it go. Another took it to the ocean, tied a weight to it, and watched it fall into the depths. Whatever you do is okay—do it!

Shortly after I started my practice, a female client came to me because she felt like she was enclosing herself in her house. She didn't feel safe leaving her house and found that she made excuses to stay there even when she was invited by people she had known and trusted for years. She didn't want to go anywhere. If she absolutely had to go someplace, she wouldn't go unless someone she trusted was going with her and driving her there. She was just miserable. She felt everyone was looking at her and saying things about her. She would wear layers of clothing to have that baggy look, so no one would notice her. She installed new doors without windows, drapes and shades on all her windows that were drawn at all times. She had every light in the house on at all times. Family had to call before going to see her because she would not open the door unless she knew who was at the door. She changed her clothing numerous times a day and showered before each change so she wouldn't have a scent that might attract others to notice her. She hated who she had become.

Over time and with a lot of soul searching, her confidence and trust in self and others started to grow, she confided that when she was younger, she was a fun-loving, free-spirited person and loved to be away from her home and with others. She especially liked being with her female cousin that was her age and who she described her as a protector. As the floodgates opened, she told me about the abuse that started at the age of eight until well into her teens. Her mom's live in boyfriend was the perpetrator. He would wait until mom went away, then he would do whatever he wanted to do, or have her do what he wanted done. At first, he was a smooth talker. He would tell her how pretty she was and how lucky she was to have him and her mom in her life. He would find ways to get close to her, touch her, and tell her that he was preparing her for life so she would be a great wife to some special man. Of course, he only did this when he could do it without her mom hearing him or being around. He would tell her that it was okay to do the things she was doing because mom said it was okay to do it. But, if she told on him, he would be mean and angry to her and her mom. When she complied, he would buy her gifts—extravagant ones, jewelry, clothing, even a pony. She kept quiet and put up with the abuse.

Like my male client, she would just go into her head during the abuse and not be a part of it. As time went on and the abuse became more commonplace as well as bazaar, she became more withdrawn from everyone. She would beg her mom to take her with her when she went out. Each time she didn't get to go, the abuse continued. He played so many mind games that she got to the point that she would just stay in her room. This made his mission easy and rewarding and hers a living hell of repeated abuses.

When she started dating, she was attracted to men that were quiet, shy, and in many ways reclusive. In today's terms, these men might be referred to as loners. She avoided those that were strong willed, controlling personalities. By choosing loners she felt more in control of how she wanted to be treated. This just added to her pain. She felt she had to sleep with her dates to be accepted and loved. In her own words, she hated who she had become. She would go out with boys, sleep with them, and then come home to be abused by the live in boyfriend. He would abuse her at every turn. He started calling her a whore and told her how ugly and stupid she was. If she refused to have sex with him, he would, or would threaten to, harm her mom. This went on for years. Her life was miserable.

Then, she met her Prince Charming. He was quiet, reclusive, and enjoyed being by himself. They were perfect for each other. As you would guess, she satisfied him at all costs to keep him and soon she became pregnant. She was a teen at the time, a senior in school. She also was terrified that anyone would find out she was pregnant—especially her mom. She wore oversize clothing to hide her tummy. She didn't have any pre-natal care, and kept her secret safe from everyone until after the baby was born in her bedroom with her alone. Her Mom was furious—how could she do this to them? How could she shame the family name? Mom found out who the father was and contacted him immediately.

He was thrilled. He had moved to Texas, but rushed home to be with them. He married her immediately and took responsibility for the child. He moved his new family with him to Texas where they stayed for a few years. This stopped the abuse back home. She never spoke to her husband about the abuse of the past. She kept it as her secret and hoped to live happily ever after. Unfortunately, her husband had a hard time getting employment. He stopped looking for employment because of no skills and too much rejection. Soon, they went on welfare, and things got worse from there. She became more of a recluse as well. She did everything by herself, which added to her insecurity and flashbacks. Needless to say, they lost everything and had to move back to home. They moved in with her mom and mom's same abusive boyfriend. Guess what? He tried to start up where he left off.

This time she was more emotionally strong. She told him that she would tell her husband, who was quite a bit bigger than he was, if he didn't leave her alone. As years went by, good changes occurred. The live-in boyfriend as well as her mom passed away. They moved on to welfare project apartments, then to regular apartments, and finally a home. Her husband was able to get technical training and attained gainful employment. He became a good husband, father, and provider to the family. Yet, in her words, she just continued to feel different from other people and "afraid of her shadow." She described in a couple of sessions, how she would jump at sounds that weren't there or look out the window as if someone was outside. Her husband would reassure her that no one was there, but she continued to be hyper-vigilant.

Finally, she was convinced that if she talked about her past to her husband these feelings in time would go away. On their twentieth wedding anniversary, she told her husband what her life was like as a child. She explained how she feared he would leave her if he ever found out the real story. What she found out was that he was very supportive of her and urged her to get counseling. That is when I started seeing her. After much reassurance, self-esteem building, modeling, and practicing the coping skills of a survivor, she has done quite well. On occasion, she can now go out of the house alone. She still suffers flashbacks and is still hyper-vigilant at all times. But, she is better and continues to improve. Now, we are working on interventions to put closure to her traumas. The interventions that seem to work well for her are journaling her true feelings in a notebook, revisiting these feelings after a few weeks to see if they are still as painful. If so, she journals more, if not, she puts closure to the feelings in different ways. Some examples are shredding the papers, tearing them up, burning them, burying them, or even tying them to a helium balloon and letting it go.

In the movie, *Forrest Gump* (1986, Winston Groom), there was a girl that Forrest loved from childhood through adulthood. Her name was Jenny. Throughout the movie Jenny was depicted as sexually abused, as a child she was abused by her father and as an adult by many other men. Jenny struggled desperately trying to find a way to be accepted by anyone. Because of her abuse, her view of life was skewed and unbalanced. Jenny's perception of life was one of hopelessness, rebellion, and denial. She couldn't trust anyone for fear that she would be further abused. The only person she felt she could drop her boundaries around was Forrest. He was unassuming and non-judgmental to her. Around him she was safe to be herself. As middle age adults, Forrest took her into his home and showed her love, respect, and empathy until her dying day. He choose not to bring up the past knowing it would further hurt her. Even in this movie the trauma was depicted as so hurtful and traumatic that it took Jenny a life time to finally relax her boundaries.

THE CHANGE IN YOU AFFECTS THE CHANGE IN OTHERS

If you don't try to make changes in yourself, nothing will change around you.

In order to be safe, you must be proactive not reactive. Proactive means thinking ahead and planning. Reactive means reacting to a situation without thinking or planning ahead. Which are you most like—proactive or reactive? If you are proactive, you have boundaries. With boundaries you have a means of protecting yourself. All living things must have boundaries. There are basically three types of boundaries;

1. Closed: *I said, No!*
2. Semi-Permeable: *Well, maybe*
3. Permeable *Yes, okay, I will*

Let's look at a simple pet dog's boundaries. I have a full grown, 7 pound terrier named Peanut. When you first meet her she is a little reluctant to come to you. She may even bark at you or run from you. If you approach her in a menacing manner, she may bear her teeth; raise her hackles, snarl, snap, etc. Her guard is up, and you had better heed her warnings or she will snap at you, run away, or hide from you. This would be her closed boundary. I always thought she was protecting me from you. I found out that she is only protecting her chew bones and toys, so much for my sense of security and safety.

If you talk reassuringly to her and walk slowly to her, she will meet you half way as soon as she feels safe around you. This may take some time and coaxing with patience. She may allow you to touch her gently at arm's length. This would be her semi-permeable boundary.

After she knows you are safe and she is safe, she will roll over and let you rub the vulnerable underside of her tummy. This is complete submission and trust, her open boundary. Can you think of humans that act this way?

Keep in mind that this boundary can change to a closed boundary in the blink of an eye if safety is breached. Peanut keeps an eye on you for any change in your demeanor. If you appear to be unsafe, hostile, or make a move to control or hurt her, she will close the boundary and take a defensive stance. Wouldn't you? Can you think of a time you did this to someone?

Everything is safe, no fear. She will become your best friend and allow you to play with her toys as long as she gets to chase them over and over or tug with you on her favorite sock.

We as humans usually do the same thing in what we perceive as safe situations. We call it dropping our guard or letting our guard down. This is when we have fun, do silly things, or try new things without fear of making a fool of ourselves. This is where we wish we could be all the time.

My daughter Shannon is a good example of boundaries. This past Halloween season, a male high school friend of hers invited her to go with him and another couple to a local 'haunted laboratory.' Shannon asked if it would be okay. My wife and I didn't see any problems with it but, I advised her to be cautious. I was concerned that she had been in martial arts for the past seven years. Shannon is very good at it and is skilled in reaction techniques, and she had never been to anything haunted. Well, within minutes of her arrival, one of the characters reached out and brushed Shannon. This startled her, she turned and hit him in the forehead, denting his mask and knocking him down. Totally embarrassed, she helped him up and checked him to be sure he was okay, which he was. The manager on duty escorted Shannon and her friends out after only being there two minutes. When she called me, all I asked was whether it was assault or self-defense.

We can have all three boundaries and interchange them regularly. We can even get stuck in one of them.

People with closed boundaries are unapproachable. They are distant, secretive, and have an air of superiority or inferiority. When you approach them, they rebuff you or turn away. They may even be cold and calloused. The only people that they will be with are ones that they can dominate or have them serve them in some way; otherwise they will stay by themselves. They would be the villains in a movie. Lauren Weisberger's *The Devil wears Prada* (2003) would be a prime example of this type person. The villain was Meryl Streep, whom you loved to hate. She did what it took to be the best and made sure all around her were fearful of her and her actions. If they weren't, they were gone.

Semi-permeable people are a mix of both. They know when they feel threatened, and they know when to drop their guard to be soft and gentle. In a movie, they would be the hero. Which one is most like you? David Keopp's *Spiderman* (2002) would be a good example of a well rounded individual who is grounded in family, joy, peace, yet defeats anyone that goes against *values* or *laws*.

People with open boundaries are the people who never guard themselves. They are susceptible to abusive situations and always wonder why people take advantage of them. An example of this type of abuse would be in the movie, *Ella Enchanted* from Disney.

The lead character is under a wicked spell to do whatever others tell her to do even if she knew she shouldn't. Because of these open boundaries, she was taken advantage of by everyone she encountered. At times, the audience found this to be humorous, but as the movie went on her perils became very sad and almost ended in tragedy. Once the spell was broken by her will to not be used anymore, she set her boundaries that she used to protect herself and insure her safety. All things went well and she lived happily ever after with her true love.

Remember, *the change in you affects change in others.* You may not be able to change the others, but you will recognize more quickly what the others boundaries look like.

Here is a good therapeutic way to practice the above. The next time you go to a mall, take time to observe the people. See if you can pick out the people that have closed, semi-permeable, or open boundaries. Better yet, sit down on a bench with someone there and slowly move toward them. You will be able to tell right away. Closed, they will get up and leave. Semi-permeable, they will move away from you on the same bench. Open, they will start up a conversation or join in yours.

Safety is an important and a strong foundation to balance. Make sure you have it.

I love when two clients come in, and one says about the other; change or fix them! How about changing you?

Safety is one issue that causes the foundation of the leg to be weak or strong. Without safety, you have no stability. Self-esteem, how you perceive you, is severely impacted by a lack of safety. One feels vulnerable to the world—even to the point of not wanting to be a part of the world as a social member for fear that they will be injured emotionally, physically, or in many other ways. It goes to show, that even when one fears for their safety, they may not want to change the situation.

Think about this, if you want to be thin do you wait for others to diet? Do you wait for others to exercise to make yourself fit? Do you wait for others to like you before you do things for them to know you? Do you wait for others to remove your safety before you fear them? Or, do you educate yourself on how to recognize people or actions that are unsafe?

THE BALANCE
OF RESPECT

espect is such a small word with such a large meaning. Respect can be defined as showing consideration or esteem. Wars have been fought for it. Families have been destroyed for a lack of it. Poems have been written about it, and songs have been sung to it.

Aretha Franklin, a blues singer, sold millions of copies of the song "Respect" (1965), written by, Otis Redding. Respect is a double edge sword. To have it, one feels warm and fuzzy. To give it one feels humbled. To be without it, one feels unappreciated or disrespected.

Even in the smallest of the animal kingdoms there is a pecking order. If one is out of line, they are soon put back in line. Respect is very important. Without it, a relationship is doomed to fail.

Emotional Abuse: power and control, rejecting, degrading, terrorizing, isolating, corrupting, and denying.

Emotional abuse seems to have no age limit. It can be manifested by young individuals as well as older ones. In schools, we call them bullies. As we get older, we change the terminology to being perpetrators and victims. Either way the emotional scars are life-long.

Another client was a highly disciplined person who is a master of the martial arts. As a child, he was devastated by his father's refusal to give him praise for his accomplishments. His father never said, "Good job," or "I'm proud of you." His father would look for the errors that he made and point them out. He would call him names, ignore him, and compare him to others. He avoided all his tournaments and found ways to humiliate him when the chance arose. Soon, my client started to doubt himself. Even as a champion, he felt he was a loser. These emotional scars carried on into his adult life. He never married, had children, or tried to excel in his personal life. He felt he was never good enough for anyone to love, yet alone like.

Soon he was in a severe depression, became a danger to himself as well as others around him. He bought into the pseudo fact that he was a loser. He was always looked upon as a troublemaker. He would drive people that were close to him away. This did nothing more than feed his depression. Finally, his nephew, who was also a master at the martial arts and idolized him, begged him to see a therapist. He agreed to call one to stop the nephew from pestering him. He went through counselors one after the other. None of the therapists offered him a solution to his issues. When he came to me, he expected nothing except more adversity. We hit it off very well. In time, as his esteem and confidence grew, he was able to discuss the above issues and arrive at solutions. He laid out plans to reach important goals like finishing his college degree and starting his own business. He worked hard on his weakness of being stuck in the past. I refer to this as trying to swim in mud. The more you try the deeper and more fatigued you become. The only time one should visit the past is to remember good things, fun things. When we reflect on the bad things is when we get stuck in the mud.

I know we all do this, and the reason we do it is simple. We do it because we know the ending. That is why we watch movies over and over or read a book more than once; we know how it ends. It is comfy, even if it isn't a good thing. Many times I ask a reflective question to get you thinking.

1.	Can you fix the past?	No, because it is gone.
2.	Can you fix the present?	Yes, because we live in the present.
3.	Can you fix the future?	No, because we aren't promised a future.
		We can only plan for the future.

A wise old man, (my dad), once told me, "The past is for *reference* not *residence.*"

Once my client saw how he kept getting stuck he worked hard at living in the present and planning for the future. At this point, he was changing what kept getting him in trouble. He immediately stopped swimming in mud and recognized when he was slipping back.

Today, he is doing well. He takes medication for depression, attends therapy as needed, finished his college degree, and has a career helping people in need. He has become more involved in his martial arts school as a very loving, genuine, teacher. He also went back to his church and has a new found faith.

Emotional abuse can start at any age. In many cases, the abuse starts by someone you trust. It could be a brother, sister, parent, relative, etc. It may then be built upon by others outside of the trusted circle. Emotional abuse may start as little things, pointing out a flaw, tearing down a joy, picking on you or another person you care about. Emotional abuse shakes and then tears down self-esteem, which is how you feel about yourself and how you perceive others see you. Emotional abuse in many ways is an invisible pain. Some people put on a facade to hide the abuse. They may seem like caring, over protecting, sheltering individuals. They may also present as just the opposite, not getting involved in anything, anxious, "wall flowers."

The best person to portray an emotionally abused individual would be Darth Vader from the George Lucas *Star Wars* (1977) movies. He wasn't always a villain. Remember, he started out as a kind, loving child. It was through emotional abuse that he became what he was in his final years.

A middle-aged woman, who was very aristocratic, came to me totally broken because she had given her entire being to a relationship. She felt that this was the man of her life. They shared the same dreams, goals, likes, dislikes, hobbies, music, and on and on. In her eyes, this was a relationship made in heaven. They hated being apart. When they were apart, it was exciting to plan what to do when they saw each other again. This warm, fuzzy, relationship went on like a fairy tale. He was the knight in shining armor, and she was the fairy princess. They would go visit her adult children, and soon they fell for him as well. The grandchildren loved him—even the pets loved him. He was a perfect mate for her in their eyes and in her eyes. He was tall, dark, and handsome.

Did I say *dark?* Let me delve into that side of him. He had a side that she couldn't quite get a handle on. He never wanted to talk about his past. When she would approach this topic, he would laugh it off and dismiss her nosiness. If she pressed the issue, he would get stern, quiet, and leave for home shortly thereafter. Remember the pecking order? As the relationship went on, he would have a habit of saying he would call her at such and such a time and not do it, keeping her waiting. When she would ask him about this, he would say he forgot or he was busy or make up some other excuse. He would then do something nice to keep her happy. He would buy her flowers; send a card; and take her to dinner, a play or movie. He went less and less to her children's homes. He would make up an excuse that he had work to do or he wasn't feeling well.

At first when they were dating, she could go over to his house anytime and surprise him with dinner or whatever. As time went on, she was instructed to call ahead of time to be sure he was there.

One time, she went to his house unexpected. He met her at the door and was furious. He told her that she broke a rule and disrespected his request. Sternly, he told her to go home and slammed the door in her face. He didn't call her or return her calls for a couple of weeks. From that point on, she complied with his wishes, rules, or boundaries. All things went well for a while. He would call; she would run. She then noticed a new behavior that made her uncomfortable. He started to correct her a lot. How she dressed, talked, ate, and behaved in public. He even criticized how she slept. Next, was how inept she was at sex and personal hygiene, and how old she was looking. He was brutal to her in private and soon in public. After she would bring this to his attention, he would buy her presents to appease her. She started to justify his actions by feeling that he must be under a lot of stress, and she was his sounding board. It was okay with her; she could take it—she loved him. The summer was delightful; they traveled all over, to the mountains, beach, and faraway lands. It was a fairytale with rainbows and where lollipop dreams come true. Love was bubbling and brewing!

At Christmas, she felt that the time was right for her to discuss marriage with him. He said that was a good idea and she could plan for it. She was head over heels in love with excitement. She bought her marital gown, picked her bridesmaids, picked a hall, and even found a perfect ring, which she put a down payment on. As he would say to her, he was never really interested in the trivial stuff. When she would bring preparation ideas up, he changed the subject or didn't acknowledge her interest. He didn't want to look for the tux, look at invitations, etc. Are you getting a hint here?

She planned everything and did all the running. Her kids were excited for her; her grandchildren were to be in the wedding. She had waited a long time for this occasion.

Six weeks before the wedding date, she and her perfect mate were attending an out-of-state wedding they had driven to. While they were at the dinner table and the time seemed right, she wanted to discuss her final wedding plans with him. He got furious, stood up, and told her he needed to go outside and cool down. She sat there waiting for him to return. Forty-five minutes went by; she went outside looking for him. He was nowhere to be found, nor was the car. She was abandoned, but she again justified it, thinking he was just having a tantrum. She asked a friend to take her back to the hotel where they were staying. When she arrived to their room, she found the place in disarray, her clothing all over the place, and he and his clothing gone. To make matters worse, her purse, with her money and credit card were in his car. Of course, he didn't pay for the room, and she had to call her daughter, who lived hours away. She needed help to pay for the room and find a way home. Her daughter and son-in-law came to get her. While waiting, she tried to call him numerous times, with no response.

When she arrived back home, she got in her car and drove to his house. She was furious, hurt, and above all, she felt betrayed and disrespected. He wasn't home. For several days, she called, went to his home, and even called his work, but he wouldn't respond. She started to feel like a stalker. She drove by at every opportunity, but to no avail—he wasn't there. One day at work, her purse was delivered by currier. This even made her angrier. No calls, no apology, nothing—it was like he had fallen off the face of the earth. Finally, after a couple of weeks, he called her to inform her that they were done. He said he didn't feel they had anything in common any longer, and he just wanted to part in an amicable way. He even went as far as to say he had *commitment phobia* and was going to see a doctor to see if he could get help.

She was even more furious, which turned to a hurt that she couldn't begin to deal with. This is when she came to see me. She was in tears at the drop of a hat. She stopped seeing her kids, leaving the house, or even leaving her bedroom. She was broken from the disrespect that he had done to her. She hired a private investigator to see if there was something she was missing. There was! She found out that he had been dating another girl at the same time he was with her. When she informed me of this, I felt our work was cut out for us. Her self-esteem was destroyed. She was severely depressed, and in her words, had nothing to live for.

As a therapist, I have the obligation to go to any extreme to keep my clients safe. I am mandated by law that if a client states that she is going to hurt herself, hurt someone else, or someone is going to hurt her. I have to pass this information on to a higher authority. After assessing the client, I felt pretty confident that she was not going to do harm to herself or him. I did strongly recommend that she see her family physician the next day concerning her depression, which she did. With her approval, I made contact with her daughter to keep an eye on her mom. Her physician started her on anti-depression medication immediately. We began working on the issues of depression, abandonment, relationship boundaries, self-esteem, and numerous other problems.

As a therapist, I ask for content, tell me the honest story, and I look for process, what caused this to happen and what can be done to not have it repeat again.

As stability grew, we started to dig into the cause of her problem. We found out that she had permitted this behavior. She had learned as a child from her own dad and mom. Her dad treated her mom this way. Her brother treated his wife this way, and her son, just being a newlywed, was starting to treat his wife this way. Does the apple fall far from the tree? Here we go again; the change in you affects the change in others.

We worked very hard to establish strategies to combat the issues. She applied what she helped design and today she is doing well. She still has days where she thinks of him and cries or hates him, but these days are getting more distant. Each day she continues to work on closure. She has written him a letter about her feelings. She hasn't mailed it yet, and may never mail it, but she did get the pain on paper, which helps to get it out of the mind and, hopefully, the heart. She has shredded his pictures, sold or gotten rid of his gifts, and focused herself on her grandchildren and family. She is putting the pieces back together little by little. She hasn't opened herself for dating or even started to look for a date. She is bitter, and the only way she will attain the desire to date again, is to set her boundaries, identify those qualities, or lack thereof, of the type of man she wants and realize not to be hurt again. She is a very strong woman with the will to go on, with caution.

Emotional abuse: The ability to inflict severe, long lasting pain without physical violence. To be verbally abused or verbally threatened.

Without Respect, Emotional abuse will be used on the unsuspecting.

This is the most severe type of abuse. In most cases, it leaves no physical marks, but the damage that is done may be irreparable. Have you ever heard, "Sticks and stones may break my bones, but words will never hurt me"? The truth is that sticks and stones may break your bones, but words hurt forever. I can't count the times that I have had clients come to my office with emotional scars so deep and devastating that it is amazing to me they can even function at all. I have seen the biggest, toughest, wealthiest, and most powerful people cry like babies when addressing and accepting the emotional abuse they went through.

I had one client who was so emotionally abused by her husband that when she came to see me she couldn't even hold her head up or look me in the eye. She was a total wreck. She suffered from numerous physical ailments—fibromyalgia, chronic fatigue syndrome, irritable bowel syndrome, and facial tics. She also had heart ailments, chronic depression, and numerous phobias. The first time I saw her, she arrived quite early. The first words out of her mouth were that she felt sorry for her husband of twenty-five years. He was filing for a divorce because she was just too messed up for him, and he found another girl, twenty years younger, that wasn't in as bad of shape. She told me how she had two children, one grown adult girl, and one that was a teen. He told her she could have the children, and he would provide the money to help them. He moved out of the house, into one of the houses he owned, and set up housekeeping with his new girlfriend. This was all done in a weekend. He left her totally broke and devastated.

As we talked, she divulged to me of all the emotional abuse that she went through from day one. He married her after she was pregnant with their first daughter. He claimed he was trapped into the marriage, and he would get even with her in time. He played a lot of emotional games on her. He conveniently forgot any special days like her birthday, Mother's Day, and anniversaries. Yet, he would take all she gave, bought, or made him. Then tell her all the flaws those things had. He would point out her flaws to the children, friends, family members, or anyone. He expressed how dumb she was, how fat she has become, how old she looked, or how her hair wasn't the way he liked it, and so on. He was verbally brutal, yet never physical with her. After time, she started to buy into his emotional abuse. She started to feel ugly, fat, stupid, etc. She also started to manifest physical signs on her being, a twitch in her face, an eye twitch that started under stress, stomach pains, sleeplessness, and total inadequacy in her life. She was afraid of everything including sex. When he would approach her, she would get shaky and at times physically ill. She has been in therapy for a few years, she has come a long way, but still has a long way to go. He is out of the picture for now, doesn't have much to do with the teen, and is on to another woman at this writing. She has been dating a wonderful man that cherishes the ground she walks on. He treats her with Respect and a genuine LOVE. Rumor has it there may be wedding bells in the near future.

RESPECT HAS NO BOUNDARIES

A young mother called to set up an appointment to come in and see me. She stated she has two young children, a girl age seven and a boy five. She wanted help in getting her marriage growing to a happier level. She wanted it to be better than it was right now. She stated her marriage had become stale and strained.

In the beginning of their relationship, it was love at first sight. He was the football hero; she was the head cheerleader. They were meant to be forever. They dated all through high school. If she wanted to date others, he would beat up anyone that even looked at her. They married upon graduation. He became a fireman, and she described herself as a housewife (only). As I listened, I could see the white picket fence and smell the apple pies, etc. All was great for the first few months, and then she started to feel like he wanted to control her every move. He would hide the car keys or take the car. He would make sure he called her many times during the day, "Just to check in!" He would call wherever she was; he made sure she had a cell phone at all times, in case "he needed something."

Are you starting to get the idea or hint here? I asked her if she just didn't answer his call what would happen. At first, she said she always answered his call. Then she said, chuckling a little, that she just didn't feel like talking and let it ring. He had ways of finding out where she was. On one occasion, he knew she was at his mom's house. He was at the fire station on duty. He left the station, telling the chief he had to go home because he felt there might be an emergency at home. He rushed into his mom's house, grabbed his wife by the arm, and screamed at her for not answering the phone. He scared her to death, leaving a bruise where he held her arm as a reminder to never ignore him again. As she put it, she felt very disrespected and unsafe around him for a long time. She stated that he would punish her often for getting out of line by ignoring her with "the cold shoulder."

Within the first year, she became pregnant. He treated her like a queen, showering her with flowers, gifts, and other trinkets. She was the mother of his child. When *his* baby was born a girl, he was disappointed and let her know this. He wanted a boy to carry on the family name. He couldn't play ball with a girl, teach her to fish and hunt, or any of those other manly things. As soon as she could, he wanted to start trying for a boy. He started to drink a lot more, stay out later with his buddies, and not tend to business around the home. She was to take care of "the daughter" as he would refer to her and be sure she was available if he called. He also became more aggressive with her, pushing, shoving, yelling, and sometimes, as he called it, "play slapping," which led to crying and more bruises. One day, her mom asked about the marks on her body; she said she was just clumsy and let it go at that. She told her husband about this and from that point on he started to hit her in areas that wouldn't show. On one occasion, he went to slap the daughter for something, she stepped between them, and he hit her instead. This became a standard; anytime the daughter made a mistake, mom got hit.

When she became pregnant with the next child, a boy, he was thrilled. His dream came true, a legacy. He coddled his wife through the pregnancy. After the birth, he did everything for the child, except the unmanly things–changing diapers, feeding, burping, etc. As the boy grew, he taught him how to get his sister to do what he wanted her to do. He taught him how to hit, yell, push, pinch, and numerous other behaviors. To Dad, he never did anything wrong. Soon, the boy found out that he could manipulate his mom as well. All he had to do was tell Dad on Mom. Soon Mom complied with all his needs and wants; if she didn't, then the boy would just slap the sister. Mom became a puppet for the males of the family. By complying, Mom wouldn't get hurt, and the daughter wouldn't get slapped by the brother. Interesting twist, huh?

Mom called me at the urging of her friend that knew me. She wanted to know what she could do to make her marriage better. What would you have said?

She wanted to know what was wrong with her that she couldn't keep them happy. She wanted to know why she cried a lot more. Why she was deprived of sex, friends, and joy. Why she made her husband drink more and wasn't able to please him like she used to. Why her children wouldn't listen to her or behave at home or in public. She started to feel she was ugly. She did physical exercise for hours at a time and started to purge everything she ate in order to regain her cheerleader figure. She wanted her husband to be interested in her again and hoped her kids wouldn't be ashamed of her perceived appearance.

When I saw her, she was malnourished, her hair was falling out, and she had numerous other physical issues. I requested she see her physician the next day and get help. She agreed, and he strongly suggested she continue therapy. I met with her weekly and started to see signs of improvement in her physical as well as emotional self. Now, we felt it was the right time to get her husband in sessions with us. He would have no part of it. He said that he wasn't sick—that she was and she needed fixed.

We worked hard together, after a few sessions rebuilding self-esteem and recognizing three types of abuse, physical, sexual, and emotional. I noticed she was getting stronger and more confident. She wanted to stay longer in session, talk more, and discuss her plan of escape if he abused her again. Pack a bag of clothing, put some money aside in a safe place, make a spare set of car keys, have a trusted friend to go to or women's shelter, and know how to dial 911 even in a dark room. Reality had set in, and she feared for her safety and her children's as well.

We worked on recognizing the cycle of violence, and she began to realize what her family cycle looked like and the different stages they were in. She knew the cycle was predictable, unless she changed the cycle he would soon cause her pain or, worse yet, her kids. Sure enough, he reached the violence stage, but this time she was able to escape before he hurt anyone. She left, called 911, pressed charges, and waited to see what was going to happen. The only drawback was that her son was very angry with her. He blamed her for having his dad arrested. They stayed apart for almost a month. He convinced her that he had changed and would treat her like a queen. She bought into it. He treated her well for a few weeks, long enough for her to feel everything was going to be okay. She quit counseling. A few months later, I heard from an acquaintance that he was back to beating her and doing even more drinking and intimidating. I also heard that his son was regularly suspended from school for violence, especially to the girls as well as the female teachers. Surprise, surprise!

I will say it again: respect has no boundaries without it the balance is off.

I often hear males say, "That is a woman's job," or women say, "That is a man's job." The most successful relationships are those that work together. Respect is everyone doing everything: the wash, dishes, and floors, picking up after self or others—helping each other and being empathetic and loving.

Keep in mind Respect can show itself in different ways, so can disrespect.

A mom called me to come in and discuss her daughter who was flunking out of college because she refused to go to class. Dad agreed to move her into an apartment because she convinced him that the dorm was too noisy and impeded her studies. He also felt good knowing that she would be moving into an apartment with other girls from college.

Let the fun begin—they partied, drugged, drank, and each had numerous sexual partners that they shared unconditionally. By the way, this was her freshmen year, first semester. The parents paid for everything. They supplied her with spending money and a credit card for expenses. When their first bill arrived in the mail, she had run up five thousand dollars in fun. When the dad drove to see her unannounced, she was very cold and began to immediately making him feel guilty that she didn't have a car to get back and forth to college, and she wanted to get a part-time job at a local night club where she might make enough money to pay her own college. She pressed him hard for a car to use—not just any car but a new sports car like her friend had.

Needless to say, my next session was with both parents and their daughter to see if we could lay out a plan that everyone could work with. Mom was ready to let her fall on her face; she wanted all forms of support to stop at once and to move out of the house. She didn't care where she went or who with. *Very closed boundary.* Dad wanted her to quit school, get a job, and pay him back for everything he had spent on her. She could live at home, but she had to follow all of their rules at all times. She also must attend a local technical school as long as she lived there. *Permeable Boundary.* The daughter was appalled. How could her parents, her blood, her keepers, be so cruel, cold, and heartless? She was just trying to find herself. She stated that they had always told her to live life to the fullest and play while you are young, because when you become an adult you are to be responsible for yourself and playtime is little to none. She lived with open boundaries; she had no respect for anyone or anything, mostly herself.

After numerous sessions, a plan had been laid. I drew up a family contract, and all of them signed it with me as the witness. She would live with her grandparents and get a job. She would give her parents a fixed amount of money per paycheck until she had paid back 50 percent of what she owed. She would also pay rent to be at her grandparents' house and follow their rules. Once she had paid her debt, her parents would consider getting her a car to use while she attended local college. She would pay fifty percent of her college bill and would have to pay for any credits in which she earned a C or below. She could move back into the home to save rent money and had to agree to random drug testing. As of the last time I was with them, all was going well. She was a sophomore and maintaining good grades. She was working part-time at a local department store and showing a lot of respect for herself, others, and her family. She is dedicated to living up to her end of the contract not for her parents, but for herself. An interesting aside to this story is that she recently moved to another state that offers a fine education program in psychology and marital therapy.

How many of you have noticed a lack of respect with our children toward each other, toward adults, or those in charge of them like teachers, sitters, siblings, neighbors, coaches, etc. Where do they learn this behavior? Maybe they have learned it from their parents (or lack of), TV, radio, media, internet, and now even high-tech cell phones.

Studies have shown, books have been written on, and adults have discussed with anyone that will listen, one of the biggest evils and destroyers of families we have is today's technology. Don't get me wrong here, I firmly believe in technology; without it, we are stuck in a place of no growth. Yet, again studies have shown that video games and now cell phones have corrupted the family, as well as its values. Take for example, a video game that teaches a child it is okay to run over a person, wreck them into a wall, shoot them, and/or set them on fire to get more points to win. Win what? How about the game that teaches a child to shoot another person or thing to kill them, blood splattering, guts flying etc.—some fun, huh?

What have we done to our future adults?

By allowing them to play these games, the game makers have taught our children to completely desensitize their emotions. We have taught them that if they restart the game all is new for another killing spree. Where is the respect for life, people, humans, animals, our planet, and our universe? Look at what we have done to our children! When they shoot, run over, or maim a human on screen, will it cause them to be compassionate in real situations? Absolutely not! Statistics and research have shown that these games affect compassion and skew perceptions of reality. It affects how they perceive the world. It affects how they respect everything around them. It is highly addictive. We are a disposable society, not by need but by choice. Many of us and our families have lost the ability to respect. I have had children, teens, young adults, and adults abuse themselves to play a game. They will deprive themselves of food, water, sleep, and social interaction with others. I had one man that was so addicted that he would not go to work; he would call in so he could practice to beat his kids at a game. He was a policeman. I had a child that would sleep in his classes because he was up all night playing video games. When I called the parents, their response was, "What are we to do? Stay up all night to stop him? You can guess my answer.

Another family curse is the new high-tech cell phones. They have literally destroyed respect, communication, trust, and safety all in one. I have students that are committing suicide because of sexting, sending inappropriate pictures over the internet to each other, and cyber-bullying. Threats, lies, and gang bullying are rampant over the internet. Children are sending illicit pictures of themselves, taken by their phone cameras, to others by choice or threats of physical harm. Groups of kids are selecting one of their peers to attack on the internet and brutally defame their characters with lies and allegations.

Texting to each other has removed verbal communication with families. My wife and daughter Shannon are constantly texting people. We can be discussing something verbally, the cell- phone will make its incoming text noise and one or the other will read the text, respond with a text back to the person that sent it, and make me wait for our discussion to continue. This goes on day and night. They get offended if I yell, which I do a lot.

We need to get in touch with ourselves. We need to take time for each other, talk with each other, and sit on the porch without video games, TV, media, Internet, cell phones, texting, iPods, and anything else that may be a distraction.

In the TV show, *The Andy Griffith Show* (1960), created by Sheldon Leonard, we are given examples of how to be more like Sheriff Andy and sit on the porch with Opie, Deputy Barney, and Aunt Bea. They demonstrated how to talk and listen to each other, laugh, share their heritage, and take time to teach and receive respect.

We *must* change the direction our relationships are going before it is too late. Our leg of respect is in jeopardy. We *must* reestablish respect and family values.

Disrespect has overtaken our family, society, and world.

I had a single mom come see me with three male children ages, ten, thirteen, and sixteen. She was trying to do the best she could to pay the bills and keep a roof over their heads. She worked nights at a local fast food chain, which meant that the boys were on their own much of the time. The dad was out of the picture he was in jail for selling drugs. The oldest child had taken on the male role as a father to his brothers. The middle child was a behavior problem child with no feelings or respect for anyone in power. He made life a living hell for everyone, including himself. He had a police file for shoplifting, violence, vandalism, and numerous other issues. He was addicted to video games, internet porn sites, and terrifying his younger brother. The youngest was a very quiet child, yet quick to become outraged if he was taunted.

That brings us to the mom. She was a wreck. She didn't know what to do, or even what she was going to come home to. Recently, the oldest had found a way to stop the middle child from breaking *his* rules. He would just beat him to a pulp! Mom would come home to her house destroyed, everything a mess, both bloodied, and the youngest excited to tell what happened and how he tried to stop them from fighting by calling the mom at work numerous times. Now they came to see me!

Respect—do you think that this may be an issue here? Is safety a concern? The first thing we had to do was put the mom back in charge as the parent. It was amazing how relieved the boys were when they heard that their mom was the head of the house and that she set her rules for them to follow. She also realized that with this new responsibility came a lot more pressure on her to be the parent, not like one of the kids. I met with them weekly for many months. The end results were that the oldest finished high school and attained a scholarship in football to a local university.

The middle child was held back in school; he had to go to a juvenile detention center to get his act together for stealing, assault, and battery. Since his return, he has done pretty well but still is in a power struggle with his mom. I feel she will win. The youngest is doing very well, even though he is without a computer, Internet, and video games. He can only go to mom-approved movies, see mom-approved friends, and has a mom-mandated curfew and bedtime. Mom has also enacted a weekly game night, when her schedule permits, where all the kids join in on with their mom-approved friend or girlfriends. She said this is a wonderful life now even though the struggles are the same regarding paying the bills, and keeping a roof over their heads. Respect!

To say the least, respect is a difficult leg to build. It is easier to just ignore others, especially ones that hurt us, than it is to find ways to make it better. If we surround ourselves with disrespectful people, we will be disrespected. We have to recognize it and stop it!

How do you feel when you are respected? How do you feel when you respect others? What breaks down respect in a relationship? Lying, cheating, stealing, bullying, and, on and on. All negatives that affect or infect our being are disrespectful.

THE BALANCE
OF TRUST

Trust can be defined as confidence or faith in a person or thing; care or charge. Trust means to have confidence or faith in, to believe, to expect, to entrust, and to depend on. Trust is a five-letter word that defines an enormous amount of power. We, as humans, will have a very difficult time surviving this world without trust. Notice, I did not say we couldn't survive; we can after a certain time of nurturing.

Where does trust begin? It begins at conception in the womb. Let me explain, when my wife was pregnant with our daughter, Shannon, we decided to go on a vacation to Virginia. We were going to visit some family that we had not been with in many years. The first day there was a beautiful day. It was hot, steamy, and a perfect day to be on a boat. So off we went with family and friends to the lake where they had a thirty-foot speedboat at their dock. It cruised sixty mph with all of us in it. We bounced on the waves, skied, swam in the warm water, tubed, lay out in the sun, jumped more waves, and then decided to have a beachside picnic before we headed to their home for the night. It was an exhilarating day to say the least. It was totally a selfish day. We acted like kids. It was wonderful until we got back to the house. My wife Margaret started to feel uncomfortable. She said she hadn't felt the baby move in many hours. I tried to justify this by telling her she must be tired, and we should go to bed. At three a.m., my wife awakened me in a panic saying something was wrong. She had been awake for hours waiting for the baby to move, and it had not. We rushed her to the hospital.

In the emergency room, she was examined and had an ultra sound done. The baby's heartbeat was strong, and no unusual signs were noticed. The emergency doctor asked what we had done this day that was different from a regular day. After explaining, he said he knew exactly what was wrong. Our baby was seasick. We had given the baby a reason to not trust us. She wasn't going to move until she felt it was okay to move. Needless to say, we did not go out into any boat or on any lake until after she was born. To this day, she still gets squeamish on the water.

When we are born we are helpless. We can't do anything for ourselves. When you compare us to other animals in the world we are very dependant, immature, and at the mercy of the world. As an infant, we can't find our own food, keep ourselves clean, or keep ourselves safe from dangers. Truthfully, we can't even wipe our own bottoms until someone teaches us to do this. We depend on others. When good things happen, we learn to trust them; when bad things happen, we learn distrust.

A mother during pregnancy is usually overprotective of the child forming in the womb. They change many of their habits. They eat better, sleep more; rest, wear different clothing, and usually try to stop anything that may cause harm or trauma to their unborn child.

As a baby, we hold on to them like they are made of porcelain glass. We want this child to feel safe. As soon as it cries or makes a sound, we are there to make sure all is okay. We even have super sensitive monitors to hear them breath as they sleep. We nurture, coddle, and even spoil the baby. We keep it from harm by a stern look, voice, touch, clap, or whatever it takes to keep the child from injury. Trust is further developed.

Remember as a child, learning to ride a bike. First you had the little tricycle. Someone would hold you, push you, catch you, or tell you to slow down before you got hurt. When you had your first bike with training wheels, you were still treated somewhat like on your tricycle, but were given a little more freedom. You trusted the person who was pushing you, and you trusted that this person wouldn't do anything to endanger you. Next, the training wheels are off, you are held as you ride until the trusted person can no longer keep up with you, and they feel you are balanced and ready to ride without their support. Then you are on your own to learn the skills and abilities they tried to teach or told you about. Now you learn to trust the bike, the road or sidewalk, people around you, cars, even animals.

The story continues as you grow, you start to learn who to trust in your home, family, extended family, neighborhood, school, church, friends, acquaintances, city, state, country, world, etc. and who not to trust for some reason that you learned or heard about from someone or something. Trust is a double-edged sword. It can help build you and develop the way you perceive the world. It can also open you up to harm from others because you trust them.

As a therapist, trust is a very key element in any relationship. I refer to trust as a nurturing relationship between two people, a family, a community, etc. The word *nurturing* is very important here. To give a good example of this is done in three ways:

- A nurturing person is one who when they see you, the whole room brightens because you are there.

- A nurturing person is one that can listen to you, as if you are the most important person on the face of the earth.

- A nurturing person is one that wouldn't even think of changing you, until you decide to change things about you and they would be supportive as well as honest.

- Nurturing builds trust and gives trust a strong foundation.

- *Trust is something that is very hard to develop and can be easily destroyed.*

A young man called me and needed help in finding out what was causing him to be so distrustful of people. When he was dating, he would be obsessed by his date. He became over protective to the point of possessive. He couldn't date more than one person at a time. He would obsess with the person until she broke off the relationship. When he arrived in therapy, he had just separated from a long-term relationship and felt that she didn't trust him. He expressed defensively, and in no uncertain terms, that he never gave her reason to believe this.

When they met they both fell in love with each other. He was her Romeo, and she was his Juliet. They spent every waking moment together. When they couldn't be together, they were on the phone, writing notes, etc. To them, this was a relationship made in heaven. She filled his weaknesses and he hers. I call this, "Smother Syndrome."

They were inseparable. Most relationships go through this initial phase. It is a normal phase to want to be near an attraction. But, as time goes on, we become a little safer with each other and start to give each other some space, freedoms, and trust. He never seemed to get beyond the smother syndrome. If she was late for anything, he accused her of being with another person. He would make her account for every minute. When they were on the phone, he would ask what the sounds were in the background. When they went places, he was hyper-vigilant to see if she was looking at others or if there were men looking at her. He never confronted them, but would scream at her for being too suggestive or looking the wrong way, etc. She was at first flattered by his attention.

He was her protector. He would provide her every need, as long as it was in approval with his feelings. In reality, he became a "punishing parent" (dad) to her. He belittled her so much that she was afraid of him and his putting her in her place. This went on for a couple of years. She tired of his antics and wanted to date others, especially since she was going to college. He could not allow this betrayal. She was his possession, just like his car, sports equipment, shoes, clothing etc. He came up with a way to control her. He would have her become engaged to him. His logic was if he bought her the ring, he was invested in the relationship, and she was his property. He would then be totally in charge and her parents couldn't say anything. As a matter of fact, he could tell them what to do since she was his. His logic was he loved/owned her, and this was a way to prove it.

The girl went along with this logic. Excitedly, out they went to buy the ring on time payments. It was a very nice ring with a perfect stone and a high price. It would take a long time to pay for. But now, in his mind, he was in full control. He had the right to tell her what to do, and she had the obligation to listen—or should I say, "the duty to listen." He was the "man" of the relationship, and she was his property. All things were back in "status quo." But, just in case, he worked out a deal with a friend to buy the ring from him if things didn't work out. This way he wasn't out the money.

He signed up to go to college where she went. They took many of the same classes, using the same books, riding together to school, leaving together, eating together, and smothering together again. She "trusted" him, and he watched her like a hawk. Things went well for a while, and again the desire to see others came into play. She felt totally smothered. Her parents were pressuring her to date around to see if he was what she really wanted. Her parents didn't feel safe around him.

There was something that was making them uncomfortable. They pressured her to date others.

In order for him to be in control, the punishments had to increase. He yelled louder, intimidated her, started some minor hitting, and had anger tantrums when needed. He belittled her parents and siblings. He made her feel he was much wiser than her and that she needed to be away from them or they would ruin her life. She complied.

This went on for a while longer. Her mom started to notice her mood change; she withdrew from everything. She stayed in her room more, seemed cold to others, and was sad most of the time. When they confronted her about this, she said she was afraid of him and didn't want to be in the relationship any longer. Shortly thereafter, the relationship ended. After licking his wounds and going through the blaming process—this was where he blamed her parents and her for "ruining" his life and plans—he then moved on to the next love of his life. He had not accepted that fact that he may have some issues and behaviors that needed to be changed. The next girl was treated the same way, the pattern began again; meeting, smother syndrome, punishment, dominance, buying gifts to calm the storm, and on and on. This relationship lasted about a year. The next girl broke his pattern. This girl threw him out of her apartment when he demanded she do what he wanted and not argue with him. His reason for being demanding was because he was paying rent to live there, he had the right to tell her the rules to be with him.

When he came to me, he was a wreck. Why did he pick such troubled women? Why didn't they all do what he said and wanted? He knew what was best for them. What was wrong with them? What could he do to fix them? He exclaimed that he just couldn't trust any of them.

After meeting two times, he convinced himself that nothing was wrong with him and that he was healed and in charge. He told me that I had issues, and he didn't want to continue with therapy. He stormed out of the office, slammed the door, and exclaimed he had healed the therapist with his knowledge of life and the brain. End of story.

Trust should be a cherished balance. When trust is breached, it crumbles and falls. Its strong foundation is weakened, yet it can be rebuilt. We must learn from mistrust. We have to become stronger and more observant.

Trust is also negotiable. In business, it is referred to as "quid quo pro," "This for that," or "I will do this, if you do that." We must always put ourselves in a position of power over ourselves. If we relinquish this power, we then fall prey to the predator. What does a predator do to prey? It sets it up to dominate it and devour it. We have to be in charge and control of ourselves. We can't depend on others to tell us what to trust or not at all times. We have to go with our *internal locus of control.*

When we follow this internal guide, we depend on ourselves to be in charge and to make logical, safe decisions. If we depend on the *external locus of control,* we depend on others to tell us what to do at all time. Again, who should be in charge of you—you or the outside world?

You may be thinking at this point that the out-side world does tell you what to do. You are right, but what the outside world tells you is ways to stay safe. Examples: laws, speed limits, signs, assessments, and so on. These should be used to help guide your trust and its development, but not the only direction to follow. We, as humans, inherently want others to make decisions for us. That way, if something goes wrong, we can blame someone else for the error.

Look around. When we buy a car, we have been bombarded by advertising for that car before we even know what we want. Everything we want has had some push from somewhere to sway our thoughts. The external world tries desperately to make up our minds for us, and we will give in when we are beat down or hooked.

A middle-aged female called to get help in a relationship she was in. She explained her horoscope stated this guy was her perfect mate. To get more proof she went to a palm reader, and this professional reader confirmed he was her best bet after five one hundred dollar sessions. She next went on the Internet and took some assessments that confirmed this was the guy in a vague sort of way. She was so desperate that she was convinced that this was him. All of her girlfriends agreed; he was perfect. He was cute, tall, a good dancer, and a little flirty. He drank a little too much and had a "potty mouth," but he did take his "chew" out when he was going to kiss her. Then he put it back in his cheek.

She had noticed that he liked to be the center of attention, especially when he was on the dance floor with her. He would twirl her, dip, swoop, and other things to her. Then, when he saw her do something wrong, he would insult her and find someone else to dance with. The more he drank, the more he abused her. She felt this was a little okay, because all the stars pointed to her and him. At the end of an evening, she would drive him to her home where he would spend the night, sober up the next day, eat her food, and use her home. Then the next night, they would do it all over again. This went on for a few months, and she started to be concerned that he had some flaws; he might not be her perfect mate. Her internal locus of control was kicking in. It didn't take a lot of therapy to figure out that she was being used and why. She went to her perfect mate and tossed him out on his ear. She has since met an acquaintance that seems to be wonderful. He is loving, kind, generous, and worships the ground she walks on. He doesn't dance, which was one of her big items in life, but they are taking dancing lessons together and loving it. Negotiation and trust can make all things work well.

> There are many things in life that will capture your eye, but very few things that will capture your heart. These are the ones to pursue; these are the ones worth keeping.
>
> —Author Unknown

THE BALANCE OF COMMUNICATION

Many times we keep a scorecard in a fight. Does this fix the problem or make it worse?

Learn to talk and fight fairly. The majority of relationships fail because people stop Communicating. Once this stops the leg of communication falls. This may sound like a bold statement, but statistically and through numerous studies it has been proven over and over again to be true.

One of the approaches I use is for a couple is to rethink the last argument they had. I then have them start to discuss how they would have liked it to go.

The majority state they wish the fight wouldn't escalate into a yelling match. I had one client state his wife kept a mental scorecard every time they had a fight. When he would say something that hit a nerve, she would mark it down in her head and immediately start thinking of how to get even. What this caused is selective hearing, and she was no longer hearing the issues in full. She is thinking of a good—make that a *great*—comeback. When she got her chance, bang!—upper cut or low blow.

What I have most often encountered is that couples get caught up in the fight mode without knowing that there are rules to fighting fairly and, most importantly, that they must be followed.

Did you ever watch a boxing match? Two people step into the ring with the ability and intent to knock the others person out. Do they just go at it? No, there are judges, a referee, ring men, doctors, trainers, cut men, bell man, time keeper, and on and on. They have a certain time limit per round, and they have a fixed number of rounds per fight. In between rounds, they rest, have fluid provided to them, plan a strategy with their trusted ring manager and trainers, and think back what they have learned about the other person in the round before or while training for the fight. Even the ring is special. There is a canvas floor that is flexible, ropes to keep each other from falling out, and turn-buckles covered with rubber so no injuries can occur if they fall or hit them. There are even floor cushions if they fall out. Before the fight begins, the referee calls the fighters and their managers into the middle of the ring to go over the rules one last time. Yes, they have rules for a fair fight. If a rule is broken, there are numerous consequences, from points being deducted to being disqualified. The safety of the fighters is the utmost concern. There are even three judges to evaluate each round and score them. If there is no knockout or injury, there may be a draw, and the judges' numbers will determine the winner. This whole process is so the fight is fair and even sanctioned by the state they fight in.

What we need to do is the same thing in a verbal fight. I have seen boxers less beaten in fifteen rounds, than couples verbally fighting for one minute. Remember that stick and stones saying? *Words hurt forever!*

RULES FOR FAIR FIGHTING

1. Agree on a time. Ask permission.

2. Focus on a single gripe.

3. Agree to talk until a decision is reached that you both can live with. Listen with an open mind.

4. Take a time out but agree to come back to it.

5. Then put the problem behind you.

6. Don't hit below the belt. You are not trying to obliterate each other.

7. Stick to the present. Don't clobber with the past.

8. Speak for you, don't mind read.

9. Don't stockpile negatives.

10. Make decisions Compromise.

11. Listen to each other and provide feedback check out what you have heard. Say, "This is what I heard you say..."

12. No violence! If you yell, you are the looser of the discussion. Take responsibility and accountability for your actions.

13. Agree to disagree. It is ok to not always agree, but respect each other's views.

FOULS TO THE ABOVE RULES:

1. Name calling
2. Blaming
3. Sneering
4. Not listening
5. Getting even
6. Put downs
7. Bringing up the past
8. Threats
9. Pushing
10. Hitting
11. Bossing
12. Making excuses
13. Not taking responsibility

COMMUNICATE NOT MANIPULATE

A female called in the other day all excited that she had met a man that really made her happy. He met the qualifications of trust, respect, safety, and communication. He was her friend, and they were very compatible. I was thrilled to hear her so happy. She had been divorced for many years, raised her daughter, and had been in a few miserable relationships that she contended with over the years. She deserved to be appreciated and loved.

As we talked, she told me of all the things they had already done together. He has twin teen daughters, and they adored this woman. Their biological mom was in the picture, she had no problems with her, and as a matter of fact, they talked on the phone weekly about the girls and the upcoming holiday season. The more she talked, the more I kept waiting for her to say anything negative about the relationship. Well she finally did it. She said she was invited to a party with some of their mutual friends. She accepted and told him when the party was, where it was, and so on. The day came. They both arrived at the party in their own vehicles, because he had to work over. They went in to the party, mingled, ate, laughed, and both seemed to have a good time. He whispered in her ear that he was leaving, kissed her, and off he went. She was dumbfounded. How could he leave like that? Then she was mad, sad, and felt abandoned. She left the party awhile later, called him when she got home, and was ready to bite his head off. When he answered, he immediately apologized for his actions. He said he wasn't comfortable in party settings, but he didn't want her to feel that he didn't want to be with her. Their communication failed when she assumed that he would go to the party with her. She didn't ask him or discuss with him going to the party. In turn, he didn't want to disappoint her by not going, so he went even thought these setting made him very uncomfortable.

Now she was asking me what went wrong. Simply, she had forgotten to negotiate, and he hadn't communicated his feelings. The next time this type of situation comes up, both parties need to sit down and work out an amicable solution that both can live with. In the past, she had no decision making with her ex-husband. He decided if they would go to a party and when they would leave. She resented this and started to enjoy being at parties until the last person left. She explained this to him shortly after they met. He felt trapped at the party and wanted to leave before he said or did something that would embarrass her. So out he went.

By sitting down and negotiating, they can both be appeased. Agree that he will go, and agree on a time they will leave the occasion. Both needs are met, no hurt feelings, no surprises, no embarrassment, and no guilt for either one of them. She explained she had not thought of this; the last thing either person wanted to do was hurt feelings. By communicating, there was no manipulation. As time goes on, they can try to extend their time at the occasions. He will stay, as long as he has a framework to depend on. She will be satisfied knowing he will be with her and also each knowing the others expectations. This can turn a potentially stressful time into a relaxed fun time. Both needs have been met.

THE CHARACTERISTICS OF BAD COMMUNICATION

1. Truth– You insist you are "right" and the other person is "wrong".

2. Blame– You say that the problems is the other person's fault.

3. Martyrdom– You claim that you are an innocent victim.

4. Put down– You imply that the other person is a loser because he or she "always" or "never" does certain things.

5. Hopelessness– You give up and insist that there is no hope in trying.

6. Demandingness– You say you are entitled to better treatment but you refuse

to ask for what you want in a direct, straightforward way.

7. Denial– You insist that you don't feel angry, hurt, or sad when you really do.

8. Passive Aggressive– You pout or withdraw or say nothing. You may storm out of the room or slam doors.

9. Self Blame– Instead of dealing with the problem, you act as if you are a terrible, awful, person.

10. Helping– Instead of hearing how depressed, hurt, or angry the other person feels, you try to "solve the problem" or "help" him or her.

11. Sarcasm– Your words or tone of voice convey tension or hostility which you aren't openly acknowledging.

12. Scapegoating– You suggest that the other person has "a problem" and that you are sane, happy, and uninvolved in the conflict.

13. Defensiveness– You refuse to admit any wrongdoing or imperfection.

14. Counter Attack– Instead of acknowledging how the other person feels, you respond to their criticism by criticizing them.

15. Diversion– Instead of dealing with how you both feel in the here and now, you list grievances about past injustices

FIVE SECRETS OF EFFECTIVE COMMUNICATION

1. The Disarming Technique. You find some truth in what the other person is saying, even if you feel convinced that what they're saying is totally wrong, unreasonable, irrational, or unfair.

2. Empathy. You put yourself in the other person's shoes and try to see the world through their eyes.

    Through empathy: You paraphrase the other person's words.

    Feeling empathy: You acknowledge how they're probably feeling, given what they are saying to you.

3. Inquiry: you ask gentle, probing questions to learn what the other person is thinking and feeling.

    Self-Expression Skills

4. "I feel" statements. - You express your feelings with "I Feel" statements (such as "I feel upset") rather than with "you" statements (such as "You're wrong!" or "You are making me furious!".)

5. Stroking - You find something genuinely positive to say to the other person, even in the heat of battle. This indicates that you respect the other person, even though you may be angry with each other.

Dr. David Burns wrote in *The Feeling Good Handbook,* copyright © 1989

By not trying or practicing the rules of Fair Fighting, this is what could happen.

A young couple with two small children called to get some counseling. They wanted to save their marriage. When I first met them, I was impressed with how young they were and what a beautiful couple they made. They were both well educated, with an air of aristocracy about them. Their story was simple. They met in high school, fell in love, and married after high school. They had a baby girl right away. The wife was a mom, and the husband was the provider. Notice, I omitted the word *dad*. He worked hard as a salesman and was pretty successful at it. Soon, along came another baby. Things went well for a while until she started feeling like she was trapped in a mom role that she couldn't see any end to. She started to feel old, out of shape, tired, and very sad at the age of twenty-four.

He worked, went out with his buddies to the local pub weekly, and worked out at the gym to stay in shape. She took care of the kids and the new home. She didn't go out very often, and when she did, it was with him. It seemed when they did go out it was to where he wanted to go, not her choice. Usually they went to a restaurant with a bar to have dinner and a few drinks. They would dance to the band, drink some more, and this went on until closing time. The problem was that he drank a little too much and she was the designated driver. As the evening went on, he would get intoxicated to the point of not being able to dance, and if she danced with anyone, including their friends, he would get jealous. Things would always escalate. He would yell, belittle, and at times get into physical fights with others he thought were coming on to his wife. When they would leave the restaurant, he would belittle her some more and start all over again in the morning, if his hangover wasn't too bad.

She became tired of this and started sneaking out with her girlfriends to have fun while he was at work. She began to lie about where she was and whom she was with. As expected, he became suspicious. He started to follow her and would confront her out with her friends or later at home. This led her to be even sneakier and be quieter. The more he would complain, the more she sneaked around. Eventually she met another man at work. He treated her kindly, listened to her story, and was a friend to her. Soon, she was head over heels in lust with him. She would meet him for lunch, bake him cookies, and fuss over him. He would treat her like a queen. They went from lunch to secret meeting places for sex. They both knew it was wrong, but it added spice to her boring life and got her needs met. The more her husband pestered her the more often she would have a rendezvous.

It became a game to her. She looked forward to his bickering. She used it as a reward system. It meant she could have some fun. The last thing in her mind was to use the rules of fair fighting. Her next move was to become more belligerent toward him and his demands, almost to the point of taunting him to hit her. Finally, he did. She called the police; he was put in jail and told to stay away from the house until the case was settled. All of a sudden, he was all alone—no home, no kids, no wife, and no life. His first reaction was to get even. He wanted a way to hurt her. He wanted to take the kids away from her. How would he do it? He tried to prove her to be unfit as a mother. The judge looked at his record of violence and drinking and threw that out. Then he tried to get the kids to go against her and be mean to her because she took away their daddy. That didn't work, they kind of liked that there was no fighting in the home all the time, plus with their dad having certain times to see them, they knew when they were going to have fun. He tried a few other schemes, but none worked. Finally, he came to the realization that they needed to talk about their future, together or not, and how best to raise their children.

This all didn't happen overnight, it took a long time to get to this point. This is where I came into the picture. The first thing that had to be done was to find out what they wanted. We then had to reestablish that they were the head of the household in their children's eyes. Many times, the children are the most confused in this situation. They always wonder what they did wrong to make their dad and mom break up. How could they fix them? The children feel insecure and many times abandoned. They fear if they are bad, their mom and dad will send them away. Many times in a split relationship, I have seen the children cling to one parent or the other. They will cry when they have to leave for even a visit. I tell parents to put themselves in their kid's lives; they have lost a "normal," two-parent home, and now have two homes with parents in each. What was once "normal" is now "abnormal" to them. What they need most is to know that their dad and mom have the same rules at both homes, and they will be expected to act the same way. They also need to know that their dad and mom will talk before decisions are made that will affect both of them.

At this point, you may be thinking, why is he working with the kids here and not the parents first? I am! I am making them all communicate. I am offering strategies to re-opening the lines that can make life change. I am also an advocate of children. I will do anything I can to be sure they are safe and will grow knowing values and principles. Please remember, what these children see and live are what they will do in their own relationships.

The Balance of Communication is a balance that must always be open and never closed.

After practicing their newfound skills, it was time to start checking in on how the relationship looked. To my joy, it was progressing along well. They weren't fighting any more. They spent most of their time talking to each other about the children. The sneaking didn't matter anymore. As a matter of fact, she became tired of the person, who lied to her to get *his* needs met. Now it was time for both to work together as a couple.

Date night: We made a game of it. He had to ask her out for a date. Remember in the past he controlled the place, time, and so on? Now, it was her turn. She got to pick the time, place, and so on. He got to pay for it. She decided on an evening out to a fancy restaurant, a movie, and then home. He had to dress up and buy her flowers for their date. They were like two kids going to the prom. They were holding hands as he led her to her car and opened the door for her. I felt good about this one.

When they returned the following week, they arrived fifteen minutes early. They couldn't wait to tell me how much fun they had. They talked, laughed, and both even cried a little. They had so much fun that they decided to do it again this week. Now was time for compromise. He had to pick the restaurant and movie, and she would pay. I asked if this was agreeable, they agreed with one stipulation from her. She didn't have extra money for the food—she could pay for the movie, but he had to pay for the popcorn. They now agreed he would pay, but only if she would pick the movie! Compromise! No, I didn't make a mistake; he let her pick again. They arrived the following week like two star-struck lovers. They had a great time. Being a counselor, my job is to check how the process is working. I suggested they go out with friends to a restaurant or dance and have fun. When I said this, they looked at each other and said they had discussed this and decided that they didn't want to get back into the old habits. I asked what caused them to make this choice. I was told that the "change in them affected the change in others." They liked how they were feeling toward each other and their kids now; they didn't want to spoil it. They even missed the next week's session because they wanted to take the kids on a family adventure night, which consisted of dinner and miniature golf. Wholeheartedly, I agreed.

When they returned, they looked like a mom and dad. They brought their kids with them. We spent the session just talking and sharing. The kids were wonderful. They shared how much fun it was to have their mom and dad happy. They shared about the family night—mom hit the golf ball over the fence, and dad ran after it. They talked about the restaurant that had a big plastic mouse at the door, and video games, and pizza and, and …

Their mom and dad were in the final stages of planning when they would move back together again as a couple. They had already laid out the plans on rules of the house for them as well as the kids. They made detailed lists of who would do what chores around the house. They discussed and agreed to what night would be family night and what night would be Mom and Dad's date night. They were well on their way to rebuilding the balance of Communication.

How we are raised has a lot to do with how we communicate. I was raised in a strict Irish family. I was taught adages and statements like:

- Children are seen but not heard.
- You be careful how you say that.
- I was told to respect my elders.
- Don't talk back.
- If I didn't have anything nice to say, don't say anything at all.
- Little pictures have big ears.
- Don't you sass back.
- Don't you look at me that way.
- You stand and let the elder sit.
- You open that door and hold it for the adult.
- Let the children eat first.
- You sit at the children's table.
- Please. Thank you. May I? I appreciate.
- Please, you have this.
- You break it; you buy it.

- Clean your room.

- You can't always get what you want, but you get what you need.

- Quit your crying, or I will give you something to cry about.

- Do as I say, not as I do.

- Stand on your own two feet or someone will knock them out from under you.

One thing I was taught was values. My parents had no trouble expressing their beliefs and morals to me. They did this in two ways: verbal communication and nonverbal communication, which could be a look, sound, body language, and even a smack in the head, back, or butt, etc. I learned at an early age the difference between right and wrong, good and bad, and safe and unsafe from both types of communication. When I would do wrong, Mom had a look; she didn't have to say a word. This look could stop time. Even Dad respected her when she gave "The Look." As a matter of fact, I feel all living creatures were fearful of it. You would be relieved if it was not you she was giving it to and very concerned if it was you. My parents would always express why they were disappointed, sad, or concerned. I knew what I had done and how I had to fix it. I learned from them to not reserve my morals but to stand by them. Even today, with my own children, I use many of their *old* techniques to pass on my moral belief system. How will we as a society survive without communicating morals? Look around today. Does this world look like a giant "Jerry Springer Show" without bodyguards? Wouldn't it be wonderful if we were remembered as being virtuous, righteous, noble, ethical, and principled? By being remembered this way means we taught the basics of communication to others. When do we start communicating?

My parents did practice what they preached. They were religious people with charitable hearts. They would go to any extreme to help others. They were fair, loving, and loved people. They enjoyed family and made family first in their lives. Their communication was at times weak toward each other, but they would "fix the problem," in their own ways.

I never heard a profane word from their mouths. As they became older and had numerous physical ailments, they would unconditionally love each other in the worst of times. They never ever uttered the words, "I quit." Go over, go around, or go through, but never give up. So often I hear two words: "I quit," "I can't," "I won't," and so on. This stops communication cold.

In counseling we have two proven axioms, or belief systems.

1. One cannot not communicate
2. One cannot not change

When we aren't talking, we are talking, and when we don't want change we are still changing. Have you ever been around a person that refuses to talk? Aren't they communicating, by a look, body language, or whatever?

Quitting is the act of giving up. You go your way, and I'll go mine. Get out of my life. Leave me alone. Go away, and on and on.

Is there a time to give up? Yes, when all ways have been tried or you or your family is in critical danger.

Have we lost the ability to communicate? Could it be that we have become much more selective? We have more ways than ever to stay in touch. As a matter of fact, it is overwhelming. Some may even refer to it as "technostress." This phrase is used to describe all the ways we can be in touch with each other. Even if we try, we can't get away from each other. We have e-mail, voice mail, text mail, twitter, cell phones, fax, computers, personal satellite dishes, digital cameras, and handheld personal computers that will beam information to others. We have answering machines, call forwarding, call interruption, *67, and *69. We can be watching television and receive a message over the set. We can't even get lost with the global position systems (GPS) that our cell phones have. We can communicate to anyone anywhere in the world at any time. We can also be selective to whom we talk. We have the ability to see who is trying to reach us before we acknowledge them with caller ID—now this even shows up on my television.

When I hear, "I forgot" or "I didn't have time to get in touch with," I just shake my head. The real problem is we have lost sensitivity toward each other. We don't care enough. Think back when you were dating, what did you do most? Talk, both verbally and nonverbally to your date. You called, wrote notes, and any of the above options. You made or bought gifts, did special things for each other, and showered each other with signs of endearment. You may have even made up pet names for each other—honey, sweetie pie, lover, and so on. When was the last time you used the pet name? If it has been awhile, what caused the time lapse?

So many times people say they just won't listen. My response is, did you, or they, check to see what they heard? A good intervention is for each person to say, "This is what I heard you say." Then repeat what they heard. Many times, what was said is not what may have been heard or intended. This little exercise really helps open the lines of communication.

A movie that I feel depicts the lines of communication would be *Independence Day* (1996), directed by Roland Emmerich, who co-wrote the script with producer Dean Devlin. The aliens use our own satellite communication system to set their plan of destruction and share it with each other. It was by chance that we found this out before we were destroyed. How often do we allow chance to destroy our relationships with each other?

Communication can be used as a tool of destruction.

I met a very troubled young man several years ago. Immediately, I noticed he had a very arrogant demeanor about him. He looked tough, talked tough, acted tough, and even backed up his actions with fighting, intimidating, and aggression. He had been arrested and jailed numerous times for alcohol and violence. For some reason, he befriended me and wanted to stay in touch with me, even though I didn't make any overt signs to strike up a friendship with him. He would call me now and again to express his dislike for someone or how he had "beaten someone down into submission." I would express how wrong he was in his way of thinking and talking, and he would hang up angry. A few weeks later, he would call back again and start over with the same issues with other people. I had to stop the cycle of violence and pestering pattern. I was beginning to feel like a priest in the confessional.

One day, I got a call from him. He was so excited to tell me that he met a girl, married her, and changed his life. His new wife was pregnant with a baby girl, and he was going to be a daddy. He told me how he took a job, slowed down to drinking only on the weekends, and was a changed man. I was thrilled for him. We talked about him getting some counseling and what he should be doing as a husband and soon-to-be daddy. He seemed to be listening.

I referred him to a specialist in alcohol addiction and also gave him information on anger management groups in his area. When I hung up, I had a good feeling about him.

The next night, he called me from the local jail. After we talked, he got nervous, went drinking, got into a fight, came home, and beat his wife. Luckily, the wife and baby were okay. As we talked, he took on his arrogant role again. He began to tell me how he beat this other guy to a pulp because he looked like he needed his "a_ _ kicked." He said when he went home, his wife didn't want him to be drinking and driving, so he proved he was fine by beating her. He said each time he hit her, he would ask her how drunk he was. When she finally said he wasn't, he stopped hitting her. She called the police, who were looking for him anyway and they arrested him.

Believe it or not, they stayed together. I feel fear has a lot to do with this. They now have two children—a teen girl and a baby boy. The girl has been in juvenile institutions numerous times for truancy, fighting, drug dealing, and as a user at the age of thirteen. The little boy is a terror already and will start preschool this year. Their mom is very quiet and introverted. He explained that they were in a car accident a few years ago and his wife was severely injured. As he says, "she isn't the same in the head." He even had to go seek out other women to satisfy himself since she was in the accident and she couldn't do what he liked. He explained he had been drinking, fell asleep at the wheel, and hit a tree. He wasn't hurt, but she was because she didn't have her seat belt on tight enough.

He still fights anyone and everyone. He still drinks every day. He still "rules with an iron fist." He still states he is the head of the house. He has nothing to do with most people. His form of communication is kill or be killed. His balance of communication was built by the way he was raised. His parents were fighters, and both were chronic alcoholics. His mom was abusive to him as a child, and his dad taught him to be tough. He told me how he and his dad would trade punches to see who could take the most pain. In time, he learned how to hurt dad more to get him to quit. In time, the game stopped because dad said so.

Communication is a double-edged sword. It can help or hinder. The purpose of this chapter is to see positive ways to make the balance of communication a way to make your life wholesome, honest, and influence others to be a support to you as well as you are to them. We must use communication as a developmental tool not as a destructive one.

Remember, sticks and stones may break bones, but words hurt forever. The Balance of Communication is the foundation of yesterday, today, and tomorrow.

FRIENDS AND ACQUAINTANCES: WHO IS WHAT?

The other day, a middle-aged woman called. When I first saw her, I thought she looked to be in her late fifties or early sixties. Her affect was flat, hair unkempt, shoulders rounded, slouched over, no makeup, she looked like a grandmother that had a very hard life. I found out she was only in her middle forties. As we talked, I shared with her the balances needed for life, and I asked her which of them she felt were her biggest problems. She said all of them. She was totally bewildered on where to begin to make things better. What she was asking was which balance was the place to start.

She had chronic issues with trust, safety, respect, and communication. Her life had been miserable, and she was on the verge of just giving up totally. The only thing that seemed to keep her going was her faith and her love of her child.

She described a bad relationship, where she had gotten pregnant, and her husband was incarcerated for fifteen years to life. Her family disowned her, and she was totally abandoned and alone. She couldn't trust anyone, feel safe, and had lost all respect for herself and others. She just became numb and hardened over time. All she had was her baby. In time, she filed for divorce from him, and this seemed to be the last connection she had with anyone. She moved from where she had lived for years, got a private phone number, and just became an island. She kept to herself, raising her son, and doing the best she could. She didn't date and kept away from anyone that might hurt her.

The balance of communication is the one that most often is in need of repair. We need this balance to get to the others. If communication stops, so does all other ways we relate or connect to each other. Part of communication is how we set up our inner circle, or those we trust and can relate to. This is also known as our networking. In order for us to be successful and be able to go from one balance to the others, we have to be able to network and fill our needs. We have to be complete and not an island. This young lady was a total island, and the sharks were out there to attack at anytime she let down her guard. After discussing her feelings with her and realizing that she desperately wanted to reconnect communication. It was time to see what she had to work with. She indicated that she had a few friends and acquaintances that she felt she could reconnect with. She implied these were people she might trust and feel safe to be around.

She decided that this is where she would begin. I advised her to not contact anyone until she decided who friends were and who acquaintances were. In order to make a list of friends and another list of acquaintances, we first had to define the difference between the two types of people.

A *friend* is one that is there for you at all times in both good and bad times. They are dependable and always faithful to you. They are also willing to tell you when you are right or wrong and help you correct mistakes.

An *acquaintance* is a person that is there for you only in good times. In bad times, they disappear until good times are back. They don't commit to anything unless they gain something from the commitment.

Using the above definitions as a guide, she came back the following week with a list of ten friends and ten acquaintances. Now, we had to put them in levels of importance. We used the scale one to ten—with *ten being the best* friend or acquaintance and *one being the lowest* the person could be. Remember the higher the number the more important the person.

FRIENDS	ACQUAINTANCES
10. Anna	Shannon
9. Nancy	Michelle
8. Tori	Tina
7. Kate	Gene
6. Beth	Teri
5. Blanche	Bobbi
4. Geri	Gloria
3. Amber	Carla
2. Jeff	Paula
1. David	Wendy

This was a much harder task. Who was the level ten or five or one? Only the person could define this. Could a friend fall to an acquaintance list and vice versa? Absolutely, are they there for you at all times or only when times are good? Keep in mind that both lists are very flexible and can change even daily, weekly, monthly. Your Friend list will have much less movement as time goes on, but your acquaintance list will always have movement. Needless to say, you don't have to limit your list to ten people; it can be much more or less, this is your choice since you control the list.

After doing the above, now it is time to define expectations of the people at their different levels.

Would the expectations of friend number ten, Anna, be the same as acquaintance ten, Shannon? No, you would expect less and therefore not be as upset with the acquaintance as you should be with the friend.

How about friend level-one David and acquaintance number nine Michelle? Who would you expect more from? Friend David of course. *A friend is there for you at all times.*

How many true friends do you have? How about true acquaintances? If you see a level-one acquaintance at the mall, store, church, what are your expectations of them? Will they run up, give you a hug ask personal things? Or, will they nod, smile discuss the weather or some other superficial thing?

The question you need to ask yourself always is: Are your expectations matching your level placement?

So many times, we don't separate our friends and acquaintances. We just bunch them all together and get hurt when an acquaintance doesn't act like a friend. We draw back, possibly feeling they are out to get us. It is even worse when a friend acts like an acquaintance; our expectations are crushed. We need to keep in mind at all times, what to expect from the level they are at in our scales. If we follow this rule, we will not be hurt by those at the levels we put them.

Now you try it. Make a list of your friends and acquaintances. Put them in order of priority, ten being the highest and one the lowest on each scale. Take your time; use the definitions as your guide. When you are done with the lists, define your expectations at each level. Keep in mind that people can and will move around.

FRIENDS   ACQUAINTANCES

10. _____   _____

9. _____   _____

8. _____   _____

7. _____   _____

6. _____   _____

5. _____   _____

4. _____   _____

3. _____   _____

2. _____   _____

1. _____   _____

Getting back to my client, we chose two people that she felt would be supportive of her and she would be able to meet without feeling unsafe, guilty, or need to make excuses for her disappearing from them or them from her.

The first one she chose was her older sister, whom she loved and missed dearly. She wasn't sure where she was or even how to get in touch with her. She also felt her sister would always love her and respect her. She was able to track down her phone number and called her. When we met to discuss her conversation, she explained the conversation was a little strained. As time went on, they both started to show the compassion that brought them together. They talked for almost two hours. Her sister was delighted to hear from her. It was as if they had never been apart. She hadn't talked with her in five years. What my client found out was that her sister had moved from another state after her husband died unexpectedly. She sold her house and moved back to her hometown with her son in hopes of finding her sister. Ironically, she bought a house just a few miles from her sister. She always hoped she would run into her, but had no way of finding her, nor did she want to interfere in her life. They met for lunch and "reconnected" at the heart. Her sister was open and honest about all of her feelings and so was my client. From what I was told, it was a moment made in heaven. They call each other every day now and have become the best of friends again.

The second friend she chose was a man that had been in contact with her to just check on her from time to time. He is a member of her church and very active in church support groups. She knew he liked her, but she also knew that she was not ready to commit to anyone. She did tell me that she thought of him and always wished she could just meet with him and go to a movie, dinner, shopping, or just be sociable with him.

The next time she saw him at church; she went over to him and asked if he would go have a cup of coffee with her. He was delighted, and she was overwhelmed with his kindness and sincerity. He knew a lot about her already and said that he just wanted to help her and be a friend to her. She found out he was a widow, had three grown children, and never remarried. She expressed how much she enjoyed just being with him, and they were going to a play over the weekend.

We still meet occasionally, but it is like a different person. Each week she comes in with her head higher, her shoulders further back, and her smile even wider. She has her hair done, makeup on, her nails painted, and her image renewed. She is like a blossom in bloom. She still tries to make contact with people and establish friends and acquaintances. She has become very involved in the church social groups, and I look for her to be fine.

> Courage does not always soar; sometimes it is the quiet voice at the end of the day saying, "I will try again tomorrow."
>
> —Author unknown

DO NOT DRINK POISON

The other day, I was listening to a wonderful speaker talk about the importance of challenging each other to be the best we can be. He expressed how the longest war that man has endured wasn't in the Roman era, or the medieval times, or the Revolutionary War, World War I, World War II, Korea, Viet Nam, or the Persian Gulf. The longest war has been the war between couples and families. It is hard for people to get along. We are all different; we are all hardwired in a unique way.

I have found over the years working with people that we have a tolerance for drinking a large quantity of imaginary poison. Yet, if I ask a client to drink an imaginary glass of poison they all react in a negative way, almost like I was trying to kill them. Even when I offer to reduce the amount of poison, or its potency they still won't drink it. I finally offer a thimble full, two times a week, month, or year, and they still refuse me. When I ask them why, they all have said because it could kill them. Yet, when I ask them what causes them to hang around people that are poison to them, they shrug their shoulders or make excuses for them.

One client couldn't understand why her family rejected her unless they wanted something from her or they wanted her to do something for them. She had this happen all her life. She was invited only when absolutely necessary to any family functions. Her parents even acted this way toward her. There were ten siblings in the family, five girls and five boys. There was only twenty years difference from first to last born. She was the middle child.

As a child, she was always blamed for everything that went wrong. She had colic as a baby, was always into something as a little girl, and was rebellious as a teen. She married her high school sweetheart, had a child, and divorced after fifteen years of marriage to a very physical and emotional abusive husband. She described herself as a very "wonderful" and independent woman.

As we talked, she would tell me how much she missed being around her family. Yet, every time she was with them, she was picked on by them or ignored completely. She said it was like their job to find fault with her. After her self-esteem was totally destroyed and she felt worthless, she felt she needed help in how to handle the situation.

The first thing that had to be done was to re-establish her self-esteem. This took quite a few sessions and a lot of patience. She was totally poisoned toward herself. She didn't like herself and found no positives in her life. Her son was very disrespectful toward her and, at times, challenged her physically. She had a job that wasn't rewarding and spent long hours away from home. She was paying almost as much for the babysitter as she was making. The babysitters were her parents.

Once we were able to establish worth through realizing how much she does for others without looking for a reward, she began to accept the fact that she was a very wonderful, kind-hearted person with endless energy, respect, and love for all in her life.

Our next challenge was to identify how she got to the point of feeling worthless. What poisoned her and when did it happen? What she identified was years of abuse, poor choices, needing to be wanted, and surrounding herself with people that were takers while she was a giver. I had her make a list of friends and acquaintances. All of her friends were her immediate family. She had very few acquaintances. Next, I had her put them in order of importance. To her this was very difficult. I told her to be sure that her choices fit the qualifications of those that are there for you at all times, and those that are there for you only when times are good or for their own gain.

What she decided was that none of her chosen friends were able to fit the definitions. She finally decided these were all on her acquaintance list and low on that list as well.

She found that when she was around them, she felt very uncomfortable, drained and always on guard. She felt like she was being evaluated rather than accepted and not wanted for who she was but what she did or could do for them. Finally, in her own words, she felt like she was being poisoned over a long period of time, every time she was around them. She described that they never called her to see how she was or invite her on their shopping sprees. They just acted like she didn't exist, unless they needed something. Then they would call and try to make her feel guilty.

She came up with an experiment she wanted to try. She would stop calling her mom and sister on a daily basis to see if they would call her. After a week, no calls from them—after two weeks, still no calls. She could have been upset by this, but what she found was that she actually didn't mind not hearing about the issues of the family or their belittling each other. She actually felt better, relieved, and empowered. She no longer felt she was being bound by them and their family rules. She felt she was detoxifying, not drinking their poison.

After a month, her mom called to see if she was okay. During the chat, her mom asked if she could take her to the mall. She didn't ask anything about the family and thanked her mom for calling. Before hanging up, she informed her mom that she could not take her to the mall due to a previous engagement that she did not shed any light on. Mom called the next day to "check in" on her. My client acted the same way, didn't ask about family and cordially hung up. She finally realized that these people were acquaintances, and her expectations had to match the level they were at. She wasn't going to be hurt by them anymore, and she established true friends that weren't immediate family members.

When I saw her last, she had become the truly wonderful person she presented to me the first time we met. She had a new outlook on life, changed jobs, remarried to a man that adorers her, and recently had new little baby girl.

She was most like the Disney movie *Cinderella*. All those around her were poison, yet she was able to overcome these obstacles and find a prince that loved her for who she is and what she was. She is now "a whole person" with properly leveled friends and acquaintances, but mostly she is a wonderful person that is no longer drinking poison.

We discussed the need for her to be aware of how she presents herself to others. The way we present is how we are perceived. If you present yourself in a positive self-confident way, then this is how you will be perceived by those around you. If you present yourself in a self-conscious, fearful way, that is how you will be perceived and will be taken advantage of. If you don't feel confident, my advice is Fake it until you make it! Do you think LeBron James, two time MVP, was born with the skills he has as a professional basketball player? Confidence comes from practice.

GIVERS AND TAKERS

In our society, people refer to each other not only as friends and acquaintances but also as givers and takers. The most successful relationships and marriages are if both people are *givers*. They seem to get along better, have empathy toward each other, and work hard to please each other and those around them.

On the other hand, the most unsuccessful relationships and marriages are if both parties are *takers*. They are non-empathetic, judgmental, selfish, and advantage taking from each other at any given chance. Takers are poison to each other. They wear each other out trying to be one up on the other. Takers borrow and never pay back. They are predators that have no sympathy, and they never say they are sorry. They feel self-entitled. Takers only say, *what is in it for me?* or *what am I going to get out of it?*

Remember the movie *Jurassic Park,* by director Steven Spielberg, based on a novel written by Michael Crichton? The humans were the victims, and the prehistoric animals were the predators. The whole movie was based on the humans running, hiding, and trying to outthink the under-estimated carnivore. That is what takers and givers remind me of.

Takers can present in any way that will get them the opportunity be with a giver. They love to be with givers. They can be flamboyant socialites, or meek and humble servants to society and the down trodden. They will pull at the heart strings of the givers and lure them into their web of destruction.

They can be sweet, innocent, mindful, courteous, and so on. Their goal again is to get, not give. They are the wolves in sheep's clothing. Once they get the givers to trust them and to cherish the ground they walk on, they are indestructible and dominant. They are the royalty; the givers are the lowly slaves. Sooner or later, whenever they tire of the givers, they will drop their facade and show who they really are. This could happen right away in the relationship or later.

Givers see them as they are for a while. Givers start to feel guilty, because the taker uses guilt as a tool to keep the giver's under control. If guilt doesn't work, then intimidation may. Takers can have quick tempers or just have a demeanor that causes the giver to give up, apologize, and fall back into the giver's role. Once this happens, the takers have the givers right where they want them. The takers own them. The takers can do what they want when they want as long as they own the giver.

For some reason, givers seem attracted to takers. Maybe it's their "bad boy" image, good looks, flamboyant personality, and boldness in how they act and talk. Who knows?

Taker's only do things for the givers if they know they will get something they want. Remember, they can be smooth talkers, persuasive, entertaining, pleasing, and cunning, but they can never be givers. The takers will always be the predators. The takers are never satisfied with what they have. They always want more to impress other takers or overwhelm other givers.

Sadly, takers look at giver's as weak, sniveling, losers that deserve to be taken advantage of. Taker's can be frugal or overspend what they make. Taker's have a severe sense of entitlement that others owe them. They may feel that others are out to get them or are jealous of them. Because of these feelings, they can be distrustful of others, especially other takers and even their own givers. Taker's cannot lose or be second place. They will quit before being defeated. They will also blame the givers for losing if possible. If not, they will twist it their way so they can look like a martyr.

All this being said, most of my clients are givers. They seem to be the ones that want the relationships to succeed. If and when taker's come in, usually they want to side with the therapist, to become an equal partner with them in figuring out how to fix the giver's. When they are confronted about possibly being part of the issue, they become very defensive, loud, and aggressive, or quiet and withdrawn. They are very resistant to change unless they think of it. Usually, therapy becomes a few synergistic sessions where at first everything is presented in a third person, to depersonalize what is really happening. These meetings work pretty well when the taker's and giver's both have the opportunity to be honest and share their feelings using the rules for fair fighting. It is very interesting to hear how they met. It is almost like a movie plot. The taker's catches the eye of the giver's by the taker's actions, usually in a group or busy place. They are the loud ones or the ones with the clothing that makes them stand out. They are the ones that they look to see if everyone sees them. The givers are entranced or annoyed by them. Next, the free drink, flattery, and so on. You get the point.

For the relationship to survive, honesty and change is a must. If one party is not willing to make changes, the relationship will usually fail over time. Compromise is a must.

Taker's will immediately go out and search out new giver's to fill the void. Takers aren't alone very long, because they need to be taken care of. Giver's on the other hand, may take a much longer time to even date or discuss the "break up." Usually, they blame themselves for the failure, and their heart is wounded.

Through therapy, we work on learning the difference between being a victim and a survivor. We also work on recognizing what taker's look like and how to react to them while being a *survivor* and not a *victim.*

It is very important that the Giver's be able to be self-sufficient and not feel intimidated by anyone around them. The Giver's must also know that they can be victimized again and again if they permit themselves to be and aren't sure what the taker's look like.

Takers don't change; they become more cunning. As they get older, they work very hard to look younger—hair replacement, dye, personal trainers, plastic surgery, Botox, sporty cars, well-read on trends, and attract the younger girls.

Giver's, in general, are happier people with simple lives, need, and wants. They are generally comfortable with themselves and love helping other givers. As they get older, they are the ones that can always be depended upon and can be comfortable with a good book, a sunset, or even a rainstorm, listening to the rain hit the roof.

Which one are you? How about your significant other? How about members of your family?

A young woman called me to discuss a mistake she had made by asking her new boyfriend of six weeks to move in with her and share expenses. She had a two-bedroom apartment that she had decorated just the way she looked it. She was a very calm, neat, sensitive girl who had a good job and a very promising career. Her boyfriend met her at a bowling alley where he was a very good bowler and liked everyone to know it. He was a legend in his own mind. He saw her bowling with a girlfriend and decided he could teach her how to bowl in just a few easy lessons. He showed her his five championship rings (one on each finger, including his thumb). He was very kind, gentle, and a great teacher. He asked if he could drive her home in his new sport car, which she accepted. He walked her to her door and asked if he could see her again. She was enthralled; he was very observant of her and was also very much a gentleman. This went on for a few weeks. He didn't even try to kiss her until the third date—she was ready on the second date, but he said he didn't want her to think he was being forward. He made her dinner one night at her place. He brought all the food and dessert. She was in heaven with him around. Week six rolled around, and he asked if he could spend the night and sleep on the floor. He and his roommate, Mikey, got into a disagreement and he felt it better to leave. She invited him in without hesitation. At breakfast, which he cooked, they discussed the possibility of moving in ...

Well, he moved in while she was at work. When she came home, the place was a wreck from one end to the other. He had the DVD/VCR player unplugged because it used electricity and he had a battery-operated clock in the kitchen. He had the heat way down (fifty-five degrees), because they could just wear more clothing. He showed her his long underwear. There was a list on the refrigerator of what he bought food wise and what she bought with prices to be sure it was equal cost. He felt they could mark the milk cartons when each drank from it. He shut off her bedroom and moved all her stuff into the smaller room with his to conserve money on wasted space. He turned down the hot water tank to just barely warm and put a brick in the toilet tank to reduce water use from each flush. He wanted no paper towels, because they could wash towels at her mom's and save money. He also—you will love this—bought two-ply tissue and unrolled it, split it, and re-rolled it onto another roll to get two rolls for one.

When she called, she was mortified. She didn't want to hurt his feelings, and she may be able to give him a chance to change by her example. How would you have handled this? By the way, she found out later that it wasn't Mikey that had him leave; it was Michelle. She had enough of his nonsense.

We don't think, act, and react alike. It is very hard for us to get along all the time, but if we have trust, respect, safety, and communication, we will survive and have fun in life.

THE TEACHER
BECOMES A STUDENT

Page after page, I have been preaching trust, respect, safety, and communication. I have stressed to make your world a place of contentment and stability. Recently, I was brought to follow my own advice in a very abrupt way. I was challenged to apply the above to my real world—my love life, my career, and my everything.

In October 2007, I went to my family physician, Dr. Irwin Maseelall, for a normal checkup. Know that I trust this man with my life. I respect his integrity and insight. I feel safe with his decisions, and we have always communicated open and honestly. I shared with him that I was feeling more fatigued than normal. He also knows I am in my twentieth year since double bypass surgery. He stated I was due for my yearly stress test, and he immediately set it up for the following week. I figured I did pretty well on this since I have passed them all since surgery. That same day, Dr. Maseelall called me at work and said I needed to talk with my cardiologist immediately. I knew something was wrong. I found out I had failed the test and needed to have a heart catheterization done, which was scheduled for the next day, to see what the problem was. The catheterization went well as a test, but the results were surprising to my family and self. I had two major blockages, (97 percent each), in arteries on the back of my heart. My cardiologist, Dr. Michael Bage, conferred with the chief cardiologist/surgeon and set me up to come in the following week for stints. I was told to go home, to rest, not to work, not to worry, and just to relax.

My wife, Margaret, being the ultimate mom and nurse, saw to it I rested and did nothing. I couldn't wait for the stints to be done, just so I could get back to my normal life. The day finally came; my cardiologist had the chief cardiologist surgeon on standby to actually do the stints as soon as the catheter was in place. This is where I had to Trust and Respect their professional judgments. They wheeled me over to the cardiac surgery room, took some vials of blood, then called the surgeon to come and put the stints in. Remember, I am wide-awake during all of this. I waited and waited. Finally, I was wheeled back to the cath lab holding area and parked on the gurney. All the patients that were with me in the holding area were taken in the lab, done, and returned to the recovery room. I was getting nervous because here I lay with a catheter in my leg and no one was communicating to me what the delay was. I started to fear for my own safety. What was wrong with me? Why wasn't I being done? What were they waiting on? The nurses came in, took more blood, checked my blood pressure, and I waited some more.

After about two hours more of waiting alone, my cardiologist, along with the chief cardiologist, and my family met at my bed. The chief told me he would not do the stints today. He stated my blood work showed I had very low platelets, and he was concerned my blood wouldn't clot properly. The biggest concern was that I might bleed to death or have a severe stroke if he did them. I trusted and felt safe with his concern over my life. I just wanted to get this done and be back to work. The catheter was removed, and I was sent back home with instructions to see Dr. Maseelall the next day.

When I arrived at his office, he had already set up a team of his colleagues to see me. First was Dr. Mehool Patel, a young hematologist/oncologist. We hit it off right away. He was honest and concerned. He was very aggressive and precise in his diagnosis.

After numerous vials of blood—thirteen to be exact, and I don't like needles to begin with—there were days in outpatients testing, MRI, CT scans, ultrasounds, nuclear full body scans, bone marrow tests, and numerous other tests. The results determined that I had a very aggressive cancer of the right kidney. The cancer was eating my platelets and progressing quickly. I was sent to an Urologist Surgeon, Dr. John Wegryn, for an evaluation and to schedule for kidney and cancer removal. Dr. Wegryn was also very open and honest; he would do nothing until my heart was fixed. Dr. Bage, the cardiologist, would do nothing until the platelets were safe. The dream team was formed and I was the playing field.

Looking at this team made me realize I needed, not wanted to have The Balance of Life. In order to survive, I must have *trust, respect, safety, and communication* with all of them as a team and with each of them as an individual professional. They became my new found friends. They were to be with me 24/7, through thick and thin. They were my connection to living or dying. They were as important as my own family members. I could not have any of the above legs missing or the consequences could be fatal.

The oncologist took the lead and started me on a very aggressive regiment of strong medications and daily blood work to increase my platelets. The surgeons kept daily contact with the team to be ready when they could put in the stints and later remove the cancerous kidney. Finally, on December 19, I was able to have the stints put in. It was a little testy at times, but the chief cardiologist, Dr. Kenneth Berkovitz, did a great job reacting to some plaque that broke off and blocked an open artery causing some very uncomfortable and fearful moments. That made stint number three. As he put it after he was finished, if I would have had this done in the beginning, I would have probably stroked out. Thank you, God, for directing the hands that fixed me. *Trust, safety, respect, and communication.* I am alive!

The next day, my birthday, I was released to go home to rest and recuperate until the kidney removal. The holidays were special; I was alive. On December 26, 2007, I was informed my that sister died of liver cancer. My reality struck even harder. I had a tumor that was aggressive and my immune system was so low that I wasn't even able to see her or attend the funeral.

I had to practice my own therapy; I was having severe anxiety from all the waiting and battling daily depression as well. I found that I could improve my depression by watching comedy shows and movies, so that is what I did. My wife brought every comedy she could get her hands on and we had a laughing marathon.

After the first of the year, I was told I would be scheduled to have surgery February 1, 2008, as long as my counts continued to increase. More blood work, more medications, more tests, CAT scan, MRIs, etc.

Finally, the grand opening day, all went well; the very large tumor and damaged kidney were able to be removed all in one piece. Nothing had masticated or went to other organs. I was in the hospital three days and sent home. April 1, I resumed my job full time and have been recovering and well since.

Another setback—in August, my wife had an emergency complete hysterectomy. The surgery was touch and go but she did very well. After all of this trauma, we both realized as a couple and as individuals, we had to practice what we have learned. We had to unconditionally *trust* those that were our giving family and friends. They brought us food, helped us in our recovery and were unconditional in their service, love and patience. We had to *respect* everyone that was making the decisions for our well-being. This included the professionals that kept us both from severe traumas. We both felt a sense of *safety* from all those that were part of our lives during weakness and need. This included neighbors, friends, and extended family. We also learned to appreciate each other and all of our friends and family with all the *communication* that was given in the forms of a call, cards, letters, e-mails, texts, prescriptions, and late night calls to and from our teams of physicians. We lived first hand *the balance of life* and how delicate this balance really is. Together, we learned the importance of laughter, tears, joy, and sincerity in ways we never had experienced before.

We also learned to be more tolerant of bad moods with everyone and with each other. We openly talked about the cause of the moods. Rather than being mad at each other, we worked together to recognize how to make it better. We learned to be more open and honest to each other even if it went as far as to hurt feelings. We always talked through these tough times and still practice the *rules for fair fighting* always. We both feel this has made us even stronger as a couple and have bonded even more in our marital relationship. There are still tough days, but we continue to pray and laugh at ourselves.

Throughout all of these difficult times, I feel that I should describe how our kids reacted. I was exposed to a change in how each responded and reacted to the crises. Our oldest, Nick (thirty-one), at first he was aloof; I feel he didn't know how to react. I have always recovered from illness quickly; this wasn't moving along like usual. Nick was there for every test—sometimes a little late, but always there. He never said so, but I am sure he worked a lot of late nights to make up work. He was empathetic, sympathetic, and counseling to us all. Patience isn't one of Nick's strong suits, so this waiting kept him on edge. He was like a rock in the background that we could all lean on when needed.

There is one incident that I feel I need to share. Nick arrived when the doctor was doing the bone marrow test. It isn't a very fun test, and the instruments, especially the needle used, look almost barbaric. With enough numbing medicine, it is tolerable. Nick (six-foot-one, 230 pounds) was in the area next to me separated by a curtain. He stepped over, at the doctor's request, to see the instruments she was going to use. All I could see was his face, which went pasty pale. His only words were that he had to leave and mom was to tell him when it was over. I think he was actually green. After the test, which wasn't fun, but was tolerable, we went to breakfast. Nick only ate a little bit, and he refused to join in any conversation about the procedure with his mom and me.

He was there, good or bad, early or late. He wanted nothing except for some meals and parking, but he was a fortress to his mom and sister as well as me.

Shannon is my sixteen-year-old. When all this illness happened, she reacted in a different way. She withdrew or became very verbally mean. I decided not hide anything from her as far as my illness, nor did her mom. In November, Shannon had her seventeenth birthday with just family at a restaurant of her choice. She had a good time, but was anxious to get back home so I could rest. I was having trouble breathing at the time, and she wanted to be sure I was okay. Her grades started to fall; she slept less and was worried to death. In December, her best girlfriend's dad came down with a very aggressive cancer as well. He was given only a few months to live. Shannon saw him regularly, and watched him suffer and wither to nothing. She stayed a faithful friend till the end, but I felt it was really wearing on her and her friend's family as well as ours. Shannon's fears were their reality. Shannon's girlfriend was also very close to my wife and I, and this really strained our closeness. I was getting better and her Dad wasn't. Shannon was able to be there for all the procedures, but

I don't know what would have happened without her mom and brother there.

As I got stronger, I was able to help Shannon process what was happening. I called the school and asked her counselor to intercede for her with her instructors. They adjusted their curriculum, gave her some extended time, and showed genuine concern for her as well as us. Her grades came back up, and she made honor roll her last grading period.

I think the hardest part of the whole ordeal on Shannon was she felt forced to take on an adult role that she was not ready for. Shannon was forced to face a reality that I may die and her life would be changed dramatically forever. She didn't want to act like a child (which she was), and began to put on a front of strength to everyone that saw her. In reality, her strength was played out by her fear and anger of having no control of her life. She wouldn't allow herself to go out with friends because her mom or I may need something. She was always checking in on us, helping us, running errands to the pharmacy, doctor's office or anywhere else she could be of help. She never cried, complained or argued. What we started to see was she was complaining more about her friends, their parents, and anything else to make our family look better in her eyes.

At school, Shannon became involved in track and field. Here she was able to be an independent participant and not depend on others to win. She was also elected as captain of the school's varsity bowling team and proved herself as the best on the team. She lettered in both sports. Yet the anger was being displayed at friends and foe alike. She didn't want to talk about anything. She would come home, go to her room, do her homework, and sleep. She removed herself from many of her friends and dedicated herself to reconnecting herself to my wife and me. Finally, I was able to get her to understand her mom and I didn't need her to be in an adult role. We wanted her to be a teen, have fun with her friends and stop worrying about us. Once she felt she was able to be a teen again, she was much better.

Over time, she has turned it around totally and become the old Shannon again. Now, she just turned eighteen and is looking forward to attending college.

Thinking about the whole situation, they both had to apply trust, respect, safety and communication to people that they didn't know anything about. The only thing they knew was their parent(s) lives were in their hands. They both were excellent examples of *four: the balance of life*. They took control of what they could, through internal locus of control. They relied on others to take charge of what they couldn't, through external locus of control. They surrounded themselves with support that was giving, *friends*. They were supportive to each other and trusted those that were in charge of their family's safety. They also communicated with each other at all times.

EPILOGUE

I hope you have enjoyed this book and the interventions in it. I hope and pray that you don't give up on yourself and others. We aren't perfect in many ways, but we all have the ability to change, because the change that you make will affect the change in others forever.

If you feel you need help, please contact a therapist. If you don't feel the therapist is connecting or right for you, find another. We all need the balance of life.

Today is a present, go have fun and enjoy it.

> Never doubt that a small group of committed, thoughtful people can change the world. Indeed, it is the only thing that ever has.
>
> —Author Unknown

ABOUT THE AUTHOR

Gerard, (Jerry), born in December 1949, the youngest of seven children, five of whom died at birth due to a blood incompatibility. The first-born child was Elizabeth Brown, then four miscarriages. Due to the fact my parents were told they could not have any more children, or risk pregnancy again, they adopted Robert Brown. Through their love of family and superior belief in Gods goodness, they decided to try again. With their blind faith in hand, they devoutly *communicated* their intentions to God, *trusted* in His direction, felt totally *safe* that all would be ok. My parents showed *respect* to each others wills and belief. They wanted more children and they decided to try to have another child. I was born against all odds. My mother blood type is a positive, and I am a negative blood type. This is what caused my mother to lose five children at full term. In my early years, I was prone to numerous illnesses, croup, asthma, bronchial issues and so on. At seven years old, I was diagnosed with a very large tumor on my shinbone. The tumor was removed and my leg was saved, against most odds.

I was raised in a very loving home, but without much nurturing. My mom was sick most of my youth with heart issues and debilitating bouts of depression with long hospital stays. The medical bills were astronomical, and my dad being a very dedicated worker took two full-time jobs at Firestone and Goodyear Tire Companies as a laborer. One job was to keep the families food on the table, the other was to pay the mounting hospital bills.

Through all of this, they both never allowed their faith to be shaken. I was raised like an only child per say since my sister and brother were much older than I was. I went to a neighborhood Catholic school and attended mass every day. I always was and still am very close to God and my faith. At an early age, I felt an urging to become a priest, so in nineth grade I entered the seminary and studied for the priesthood.

At the end of my freshman year I had determined that this was not my calling. I returned home to finish my high school at a local Catholic high school. I attended The University of Akron, floundered around for a couple of quarters and worked full-time at Firestone as a tire builder. I really didn't have direction in my life. One thing I did realize was I didn't want to build tires all my life, but I also didn't want to be in college. After talking to a recruiter, I decided to join the army reserve for six years. When I returned back from active duty, I felt I had my feet grounded, so I went back to college to earn a degree in elementary education. I felt I could help kids deal with their issues because I had many of the same issues as a child that I had to deal with alone. I also loved teaching. For the next six years I taught grades six through eight in the elementary school I attended as a child. It was a dream job; I worked on my master's in school administration and became the assistant principal.

One summer day, my cousin called me while I was on summer break and asked if I would be interested in doubling my salary and come work with him at the B.F. Goodrich Company. I wasn't making much money in education, so I jumped at the opportunity. Over the next eight years I worked in business as a sales and marketing consultant. Economic times took a turn, and I found myself on a sinking ship. I was contacted by a dear friend who offered me a job as an advertising and marketing consultant for an international company that had offices throughout the world; they needed me to be a manager in the Cleveland office. I jumped at the opportunity, tripled my salary, and had the opportunity to see parts of the world I had only read about. I loved this job. I met many wonderful people, had an exciting life, and thanked God every day for all the blessings I had received. I was married, my wife became pregnant with a boy, and I was living the dream. Nice cars, nice home, money to spend, a bright future, and at the top of the game. Soon, the world would collapse.

My wife lost the baby, the trauma of this and an unhappy relationship caused the marriage to fail. The company I was with was merged with another company that wanted to reduce costs so they fired all the sales people and put their people in place. I was out of work, going through a divorce, and my health was in jeopardy. I started having chest pains, was sent by my physician for heart tests, and found that I had some major blockages in my arteries leading to my heart. Here I was, at the ripe old age of thirty-nine, needing a lifesaving, double bypass, open-heart surgery. Faith is all I had left; I also had a wonderful friend named Margaret, who strengthened my faith, nursed me back to health, and soon became the *love* of my life and wife for the past twenty years. Without this God-sent Angel, I would not be here writing these words.

During my heart surgery, I was given tainted blood, and ended up with Hepatitis D, as well as pneumonia. I was told by my physician to go on medical disability for the rest of my life and enjoy what time I had left. In the blink of an eye, I went from a lucrative life style to below poverty level. I could not get employment, and if I could have, I didn't have the stamina to do near what I was use to doing. For the next ten years, I felt worthless. All I had was my faith and my family, Margaret, my stepson, Nick, and my baby girl, Shannon.

I couldn't go on like this; I needed to do something with my life. I hated being put out to pasture. I prayed to God as hard as I ever have in my life for direction. I was at my wits' end. Margaret and I were always fighting, Nick and I were at each other's throats, and I was at a point in my life of hatred and jealousy for those that had jobs, money, happiness, and a goal.

Margaret and I decided we needed marriage counseling. The first few times we went, I wasn't truthful. I made her look like the bad person and me the victim. I was a wonderful victim. I had the therapist eating out of my hand—or so I thought. During one session, I was called into her office alone.

She looked me in the eye and said, "Get a divorce as soon as possible." She informed me that I was causing all the grief, and she felt Margaret would be better without me. She felt that I was emotionally abusive as well as a bad companion for Margaret and kids. I was mortified. The last thing I thought was that I was going to end up totally alone—live alone and die alone.

With intense therapy, a lot of love and direction, and God's inspiration, we survived this trial. I also found that I had a newly born love and need to help others. I wanted to go back to college, get my master's degree and do marriage and family therapy. The only problem was how to do it and pay for it. I was on a mission, and little did I know, so was God. I took a chance and went to the dean of the education and the counseling department and sat outside his door without an appointment. After numerous hours, I was asked to see Dr. Eli for only a few minutes. After sharing my tale, he informed me that he had a new program being offered to six graduate students, and he had one spot that had just been opened. Did I want it? I jumped at this divinely inspired opportunity. My college would be paid for as a graduate assistant, and I would have to teach classes in the college of education to undergraduates. I thought I was dreaming. God is good all the time.

Within four years, I achieved my master's of education in counseling and continued on for my license in school guidance. Within a few weeks after graduation, I was hired by the local school system as their middle school counselor, and over the past ten years, I have done marriage and family therapy for numerous clients. I feel I am pretty good at this and have had numerous success stories to share. I also want you to know, I was never in this career for the money. Most of my clients are unable to pay for counseling. I work with them; I know what it is like to be poor. Many of my clients are so confused they don't know where to begin. I work with them, because I have been there as well.

To be as blessed as I have been is a gift—each day is a gift. I cherish it. I don't know what the future holds; all I know is that I hold today and tomorrow with the eyes of a child. I accept God's light to shine brightly upon all those that are brought to my door.